# KENTUCKY CURED

# *KENTUCKY CURED*
## FIFTY YEARS IN KENTUCKY JOURNALISM

AL SMITH

Charleston London
THE History PRESS

Published by The History Press
Charleston, SC 29403
www.historypress.net



Cover photos by Steve Shaffer, Kentucky Educational Television

First published 2012

Manufactured in the United States

ISBN 978.1.60949.790.3

Library of Congress CIP data applied for.

*For Catherine, Carter and Ginny—my children who raised me while they were growing up—and Martha Helen, their editor, and mine, for life.*

# CONTENTS

# Foreword

To meet Al Smith for the first time is to feel that you have known him forever. And before your meeting is over, Al will likely know as much about you as your family does and as much about your family as you do.

It is this visceral curiosity about everything and everyone that has made Al one of the leading chroniclers of his time, that and his prodigious memory. Even more fortuitously, he is an extraordinarily talented writer and compelling speaker.

I first "friended" Al in my search for an experienced journalist who would play the key role in the launch of an independent public affairs program on Kentucky Educational Television (KET). It was 1974. KET was five years old and ready to extend its educational mission beyond the school and into the home, to inform adults even as it helped educate children. But to be perceived as credible in interpreting Kentucky affairs of state, the commentators had to be independent, not suspected of bending their views to please the powers that be.

The moderator needed to be skillful at drawing out all sides of an issue. I initiated a search at the 1974 annual convention of the Kentucky Press Association in Covington. When I got there, I sought help in identifying some prospects I might interview. As it turned out, the president-designate was one Al Smith. Even as he suggested others he thought might suit me, I realized that Al was just what I wanted, if I could get him.

Al was intrigued by the proposition, but he lived in Russellville where he was owner/publisher of the Russellville newspaper and several others in the region. Russellville is a more than three-hour drive from the KET studios in Lexington!

We discussed. We dickered. I explained that to emphasize the program's independence from KET, he would also have to produce it. He would assume complete control over the program's agenda and the choice of guests.

Al hesitated, and I certainly didn't blame him, over committing to a seven-hour round-trip drive *every* week. But in the end, he agreed to take it on.

I think he had reservations about just how much editorial rope I would give him, often testing me with a question like, "Now, you said I could do what I wanted. This is what I have in mind. Are you OK with it?" I won't say I agreed wholeheartedly every time, and early on I might have offered a suggestion or two. But when he almost never paid any attention to my suggestions, I decided he was more than worth occasional heartburn.

The essence of Al Smith is that he was born to be a public figure, in print and in person. And in one way or another, he always has been. Through his weekly exposure statewide on *Comment* he made friends as well as fans throughout Kentucky—and beyond.

Al stuck with *Comment on Kentucky* for thirty-three years with only one major absence. After five years, he took leave from KET for three years, when President Carter appointed him to be Federal Co-Chair of the Appalachian Regional Commission in Washington, D.C. Carter's reelection attempt failed, so Al served only the first year under Carter then two years under President Reagan, which certainly established his nonpartisan credentials.

After Al retired in late 2007, he decided the time had come for him to report his own story. He wrote a well-accepted book, *Wordsmith, My Life in Journalism,* published in 2011. It describes a career in journalism, and a life, that are as unique as they are universal.

He barely recovered from writer's cramps when he went to work on the present book featuring highlights of his many years of columns, editorials, sketches, profiles and history of our times.

A feature of *Comment on Kentucky* over most of its long run was the mini-essay with which Al ended each segment. If the half hour program was like a newspaper, the "go-out," as he called it, was the editorial. It became a cherished and oft-quoted element of the series. Even as this book you are about to read and enjoy preserves much of Al's many-faceted writings, he should really do at least one more that collects a selection of his unforgettable "go-outs."

There never has been enough of Al Smith to go around, to meet all the requests for his appearances, his reviews, his profiles and his company—

especially for his company. That is why these books he is writing in later life, capturing as they do the core of his thinking and being, will always be treasured by those who know him now and no less by those who will know him only through these publications.

O. Leonard Press
Founding Director of KET

# Preface

"Cured" in rural Kentucky refers to the seasoned condition of harvested tobacco ripe for market or an aged ham taken from the smokehouse and ready for slicing. Of course, when the doctor says we have recovered from a disease, we cross our fingers and hope we are cured.

In our signature whiskey business, good bourbon is labeled for sale by the number of years spent "curing" in charcoal barrels. Of someone who can't drink in moderation, "cured" used to be the cautious description for an alcoholic who seems to have quit. In Alcoholics Anonymous, however, there is no "cure," only abstinence achieved by staying sober one day at a time, accepting as fact there is no successful moderate or controlled drinking for the alcoholic. The process is called "in recovery," and it has worked for me for nearly fifty years in which I have stayed sober but never claimed to be "cured."

I lost control in a ruinous decade of increased drinking while I learned the journalism trade, with some early success, in New Orleans. I learned about "recovery" and AA's twelve-step program on a little newspaper in rural Kentucky where I got back my self-respect and rebuilt my career.

*Kentucky Cured* is not a book of sermons about drinking, but it was written by a journalist who found "recovery" and a new life away from the big city and among farm people, who value the term "cured," as in seasoned, ripe and ready. Yes, and sober—although one cynical reader told me the editorials I wrote were "a hell of a lot more interesting when you were a drunk."

The stories and commentaries you find here reflect whatever maturity and insight I earned from adventures in Kentucky journalism that took me back to the cities, even to working in Washington for two presidents of rival political parties. I came to Kentucky penniless and despondent, humiliated over my losses in Louisiana and the disappointments for my family back in Tennessee. In Kentucky, everything I once valued but lost was returned, and that which I desired was either achieved or I learned I didn't need it, in season, in its own proper time, when my perspective, at least, was cured.

The chapters that follow are a mix of opinions and narratives freshly written for this book or revised or reprinted from contributions I wrote freelance for the Louisville *Courier-Journal* and the Lexington *Herald-Leader* after I sold my own papers, a chain of small weeklies. This continues a memoir *Wordsmith: My Life in Journalism,* published in 2011, but is more about other people than myself. As the revered Kentucky laureate historian Dr. Thomas D. Clark admonished me, with a hint of a chuckle, on his deathbed at age 102, "Al, Al, nobody wants to read more than one book about one man!"

When the chapters are from the metro papers, they are dated at the beginning and identified by papers in the acknowledgements at the end of the book.

# Prologue

## Telling Sally

The renowned civic activist, champion of the environment and philanthropist Sally Brown, perhaps the richest woman in Kentucky, was ninety-six years old when I telephoned and asked if I could visit before my last Friday night show as host of the state's public television network program, *Comment on Kentucky*.

"All right," she said. "Come ahead, and I'll give you lunch."

"Well, let me warn you, Miss Sally. I'm going to ask for some money."

"That's all right, nearly everybody does," she replied.

Although I knew her slightly through our service together as trustees at Shakertown at Pleasant Hill, the historic restored village in Mercer County, between Harrodsburg and Lexington, it was only that week that officials of the Kentucky Educational Television network told me that she had sent them several large yearly checks signed "in appreciation of Al Smith's program."

Now they wanted me to ask her for over $100,000 to claim a matching federal gift for that amount on behalf of some new programs. Somewhat annoyed by this request to push myself on an old lady I hardly knew, I only agreed if KET understood that I would make a similar plea to endow a challenge match for a journalism program I had recently helped start at the University of Kentucky.

It is a rule among fundraisers to ask for just one cause at a time, but to overcome my reluctance to even make the call, the KET executives said, "Go ahead."

Very wealthy from the family's Louisville distillery business, Sally Brown shunned the ostentatious life but gave liberally for arts and education and, especially, for conservation on a national and global scale. *Courtesy of the Kentucky Educational Television network (KET).*

"Sally" was the nickname of Sara Shallenberger, who "grew up around the world" as the daughter of an army general. She settled in Kentucky when she and her new husband, W.L. Lyons Brown of the Brown whiskey family began raising a family in 1937 on what became a farm of several thousand acres on the Ohio River in Oldham County near Louisville.

Settled at a lunch of eggs goldenrod prepared by a cook who raised the free-range chickens, my hostess inquired, "How did you happen to come to Kentucky in the first place?"

"Well, after dropping out of Vanderbilt to become a journalist, I went to Louisiana, started at the bottom as a copy boy and did pretty well for a while," I said. "But I finally drank my way off two New Orleans newspapers fifty years ago, returned to our family farm in Tennessee and wound up on a little weekly paper in Russellville, not far from Nashville."

"Heh, heh!" she chortled. "In New Orleans, that's pretty serious drinking."

"It was," I admitted. "And in the state where you make all that fine whiskey, it took me five years to learn how not to drink it!"

"Check out your 1963 sales records, Miss Sally," I exclaimed jokingly through a bite of Shaker lemon pie. "That was the year I gave up Early Times. You look—I bet your profits dropped five percent!"

"Heh, heh!" she laughed again, nodding. "That was a mighty good whiskey."

An hour later, dazed by the conclusion of the visit, I stopped for a Coke at a McDonald's on the highway back to Lexington.

A half century after I reached rock bottom in Kentucky, the lady whose family made the whiskey that almost killed me in New Orleans, had just given me more than eggs goldenrod and Shaker lemon pie. Counting the matches for gifts to KET and UK, it was a $500,000 lunch.

Yes, she was still in control of her wits and her capacious pocket book. More than a sentimental personal reward to me for whipping an addiction, she was simply making another investment in her adopted state, two more gifts for the public good. She offered never-ending support of a wide range of interests in the nation as well as Kentucky: education, environmental protection, conservation, historical preservation, population control, the arts, planning, philanthropy and other facets of civic life.

Perhaps in my gratitude for recovery in Kentucky Sally Brown recognized that we were both animated by an appreciation of life's possibilities here. Whatever, she would keep on "giving back" until she "fell off her perch," her term for death, four years after that lunch, shortly after her 100th birthday.

I don't have Sally's millions to share, but the stories and comments in this little book are offered in gratitude for the career in journalism restored to me by Kentuckians, beginning with those in Logan County who took me in when I was homeless. They were written long after I found recovery through the twelve-step program of Alcoholics Anonymous. In sum, like the early settlers who came here when it was a frontier, I discovered that Kentucky is a land of the second chance.

# Part I

# *My New Kentucky Home*

# Chapter 1

# Memories of Memorial Day

There were flags and flowers for remembrance in the cemetery at Russellville, the historic and beautiful community that was my adopted hometown in Kentucky for twenty-two years. This was for the most recent Memorial Day observances at both Carrico Park Square and at American Legion Post 29, but the crowds were sparse.

Logan County is and was a sprawling region of farms—fertile on the south and hard scrabble on the north, divided by a county seat, Russellville. A tiny band of would-be secessionists declared it to be the Confederate capital of Kentucky until chased away early in the Civil War by Union troops without a shot fired. Its schools voluntarily integrated less than one hundred years later.

Russellville is on the Tennessee border, north of Nashville. The town was filled with patriotism when Josh Moore, a graduate of the county high school, was killed in Iraq in May 2007. Crowds lined the road between Lewisburg in north Logan County and around the Square in Russellville for the funeral procession. The old Highway 431 where he grew up is renamed Joshua Moore Highway. The new four-lane highway is named for NASA Astronaut Terry Wilcutt, who is also from Logan County.

Jim Turner, one of my editors long ago on the weekly *News-Democrat* and *Logan Leader*, says the local politics and speeches that we knew are gone. The last two county judge executives, both former grocers, were capable administrators but not "old school" politicians. They don't slate or put together tickets as voter guides on Election Day. They cannot

The public square in Russellville, site of an early courthouse, was round. It was beautified in the sixties after preservationists blocked a plan to cut a street through the middle to improve traffic flow. *Courtesy of Logan County Public Library.*

promise a large bloc of voters to the governor candidates they support. Democratic precinct workers no longer slip into the newspaper office print shop on hard-fought election days to seek an extra few hundred ballots for questionable purposes.

In the new century, the governor's "contact man" (the fellow to see, hopefully, to beg a favor from Frankfort) rarely makes public appearances. Turner says he is unknown to the young people who might have been Jaycees, were there still a Junior Chamber of Commerce. Things are different from when I once wrote "The Land of Logan" column in the *News-Democrat.* Fifty years ago, the national Jaycee president, Wendell Ford of Owensboro, was attracting contacts and the attention that would win him the governorship and four terms in the U.S. Senate. Ford was a Democrat, but Western Kentucky is now Republican, no longer "the Gibraltar" of the Democratic Party, as it was called in his youth.

The county seems to lack the civic go-getters who recruited industries on virtually an annual basis. With a current population of 27,000 and down to 7,000 in Russellville, most of the branch managers of the out-of-state manufacturing companies commute to work from larger towns, such as Bowling Green. The banks are not locally owned, nor are the hospital and newspaper.

Although a volunteer committee for economic development is in place, hustling new industries is entrusted to a salaried executive whose salary is paid by government agencies or private investors. Not much success with that, but the county has retained its really solid companies, including two of the largest of their kind in the country—a giant manufacturer of aluminum for beverage cans and a urethane plant for the furniture and carpet cushioning industries. The best new businesses came because the local boosters in the twentieth century convinced them our rural work force would be loyal, meaning reject unions, if treated decently. That's the way it turned out for a long time. Memories are fading of Memorial Day weekends in a colorful political era when Democratic courthouse boss Emerson "Doc" Beauchamp would send Rayburn Smith and other sweaty henchmen scurrying along narrow county roads he had blacktopped to nail down votes for next Tuesday's election.

(Political sage Edward Prichard recalled an alarmed Rayburn Smith phoning Doc to report on one election that the opposition was "stealing the Bucksville precinct." But Doc was calm. "That's all right, Rayburn—we're not counting the Bucksville precinct.")

Those who rejoice that Logan County is no longer patronage-dependent, if politically inconsequential, should decorate the graves of Marvin Stuart and Earl Davis. They were the town leaders who talked Rockwell and Emerson Electric into building plants in Russellville. Extolling the farm-trained skills of folks in a county so fertile that we grew three kinds of tobacco and other crops, Stuart and Davis pushed their neighbors to support taxes for amenities—health, schools, sewer and water lines and an airport—to make the town more appealing.

There is a lot of history in Logan County, where they number ten governors who practiced law there at different times, where Andrew Jackson fought a duel, circuit riders preached the Great Revival of 1800 and the Shakers established a colony. The citizens split in the Civil War, but, curiously, most remembered by townspeople is a wild day in 1868 when the Jesse James gang robbed a bank. With horsemen shooting blank bullets, this event is recalled in a reenactment every fall at the Logan County Tobacco and Heritage Festival.

When I got off the bus from Nashville in 1958, I was only thirty-one but couldn't care less about all this history. As the newly hired but resentful editor, I was on the downside of a decade of heavy drinking that had cost me those jobs in New Orleans. More than a bus stop, the little Russellville paper was the end of the line. Registering at a shabby old hotel on the square, I asked how to find a bootlegger. But five years later, sober and ready to tackle big-city journalism again, I had an unexpected vision of how much I owed Logan County people for transforming my life. I was changed. Instead of leaving, I bought the newspaper and stayed seventeen more years in a rural county that I came to see as a microcosm of Kentucky. I met a young woman, divorced with two small children and also in recovery, in her case, from cancer. I married Martha Helen, and we added a child, a daughter. We took a chance on each other.

This was a long way from the French Quarter. In Logan County, Kentucky, if not "cured" from my early destructive negative obsessions, they were suspended while I stayed sober for fifty years, one day at a time. I learned that when one's dreams are not circumscribed by the city limits sign, no town is too small, or too remote for personal renewal or a second chance. This is what I remember on Memorial or any other day

## *Chapter 2*

# Duel in Logan County

*May 2, 2002*

When President Thomas Jefferson's agents in Paris signed the Louisiana Purchase two hundred years ago this week, doubling the size of the country, they also opened a new era in politics, expanding the American empire westward, seizing ancestral lands of native Americans, driving foreign nations from the continent and transforming the young republic into a world power.

Historians call this era the Age of Jackson, evoking the mythic legacy of Andrew Jackson, the brawling, gun-fighting, land-speculating, frontier lawyer who whipped the British at New Orleans, chased the Spanish out of Florida, cowed or killed the Indians and became the seventh president of the United States.

Two centuries later, in the rollout of events to recall the purchase, our biggest diplomatic triumph ever, there is more for Kentuckians to remember than the journey of Meriwether Lewis and William Clark from the Falls of the Ohio to the Pacific.

A day before the running of the Kentucky Derby, one might start with the surprising outcome of a duel that Jackson fought in Kentucky over a horse race that *didn't* happen in Tennessee.

When the match at Nashville in autumn of 1805 between Jackson's famous stallion Truxton and Colonel Joseph Ervin's Plowboy was called off because Plowboy went lame, a dispute developed over terms of the forfeit

Ervin paid. Meddlers and tavern gossips fired up the issue, reviving an old story that Jackson and his wife, Rachel, had married before she was legally divorced from Kentuckian Lewis Robards. By spring, Jackson was provoked into challenging Ervin's son-in-law, Charles Dickinson, twenty-five, another hard-drinking lawyer hothead, to settle the quarrel with a duel.

Nothing could have been more foolish, for Dickinson was considered the best pistol shot in Tennessee. Thus it was that two parties of men on horseback set out to keep a date early on May 30, 1806, on what was called the "field of honor," in this case a meadow on the banks of the Red River in Logan County, twelve miles south of Russellville, on the Kentucky side of the border with Tennessee. By a gutsy decision to give Dickinson the first shot, which he knew was sure to hit him, and a strategic decision to wear a loose coat, Jackson took a bullet in his chest instead of the heart, and then shot his unnerved enemy through the stomach.

Dickinson died in agony during the night, and Nashville society was scandalized that Jackson showed no mercy to a foe rendered defenseless when his allowable one shot failed to kill Jackson. But Jackson felt no remorse. "I should have hit him," he said, "if he had shot me through the brain."

Perhaps this quarrel over a horse bet between two Tennesseans was the most fateful of all the duels fought in Kentucky. Had the odds against Jackson prevailed, historian Robert V. Remini has suggested, the first half of the nineteenth century might have been called the age of Clay, signifying the extraordinary political talents of Kentucky's Henry Clay.

Although he was ten years younger, Clay's career was similar to Jackson's. Each man moved west to seek his fortune in law and politics, Jackson from North Carolina to Nashville and Clay from Virginia to Lexington. Each married into a prominent pioneer family, sought riches in public life and land deals, became a world-famous statesman and each pursued the sporting life with horses—Jackson in races at Clover Bottom, a course near his famous home, the Hermitage, and Clay as a member of Kentucky's first jockey club, chartered in 1797 and racing on the present site of the beautiful Lexington Cemetery. A few miles from Clay's home, Ashland, this cemetery is dominated by a towering 130-foot column topped by a 12-foot statue of the great man, who died in 1852, but no words are inscribed to acknowledge that his deepest ambition, to become president of the United States, was crushed by a Tennessee rival who did.

The best-known statues of Jackson, who died in 1845, are three, nearly identical, all on a rearing, prancing horse, and depicting him reviewing his troops just before the Battle of New Orleans, on January 8, 1815. The work of Clark Mills, these were the first equestrian statues ever created in the United States.

In the Battle of New Orleans, commanding a pickup militia of four thousand Tennessee and Kentucky sharpshooters, plus Jean Lafitte's bayou smuggler-pirates and men of color who were both slave and free, Jackson slaughtered or drove back to the sea eight thousand British redcoats, a highly trained army of the most powerful nation in the world.

Without this victory, writes historian Remini, author of biographies of both Jackson and Clay, the Louisiana Purchase signed twelve years earlier might have come to naught, a scrap of paper blown away by the winds of war. Had the British won, they would have revoked Napoleon's sale to Jefferson of one million square miles for $15 million and forced the French to return New Orleans to the Spanish who had lost Louisiana to Napoleon in an 1800 surrender treaty.

While Jefferson hoped that the 1803 purchase would reduce frontier tensions over Westward expansion, Jackson's victory in 1815 resolved the question. It also gave the country back its self-respect, proved its right to independence and opened the way to building the nation. It "legalized—if conquest ever legalizes—the Louisiana Purchase," Remini writes. And it made Jackson "a popular hero for the remainder of his life."

The historians say Jackson's popularity was at the root of the venomous political rivalry with Clay, his fellow "westerner." But if Jackson legitimized the purchase and strengthened the presidency as a champion of democracy, Clay's role in our history was enormous. Political commentator George Will says he saved the union because his famous compromises over slavery in the Louisiana Purchase states stalled the Civil War. When rebel cannons finally fired at Fort Sumter, the North had amassed the industrial might—the steel, guns and railroads to transport troops—to smash the South and in the blood of thousands on both sides ratify at Appomattox Courthouse the eighteenth century Constitution of a union that neither Clay nor Jackson, although they were Southern slave owners, would have ever forsaken.

Notwithstanding the adulation of millions of Americans, the hatred between these legendary patriots was enduring. Clay said that Jackson was "ignorant, passionate, hypocritical, corrupt." On his deathbed, Jackson regretted he "didn't shoot Henry Clay."

In the early 1990s, historian Remini and I were filming a documentary about Henry Clay in the beautiful gardens at Ashland when a fierce storm came up.

Amid gusty winds, peals of thunder and flashing lightening, Remini and I dashed for shelter toward a KET film truck.

Clutching the lapels of his suit coat against the beating rain, Remini shouted at me, "I knew the general would be furious if I came to this man's house!"

*Chapter 3*

# Jobs: Marvin Stuart Counts the Cows

I discovered a tension between the Russellville boosters in the chamber of commerce on one side and the Main Street storekeepers and anxious farmers on the other when I came to Logan County to edit the weekly paper in 1958. It wasn't a "town versus gown" conflict—both church colleges founded in the nineteenth century had died in the Great Depression. It was about wages for working people.

Whereas the boosters—we also called them "boomers"—promoted visions of growth through new industries, if we could attract any, some of the merchants and many farmers worried they couldn't keep their low-paid employees if they had to compete with wages at new factories. However, they all knew that the county was losing population. The kids were leaving home for better jobs elsewhere and a brighter future.

Fortunately, Marvin Stuart, who could talk the language of hope and fear in small town America better than anyone I ever knew, prevailed on the side of growth. Stuart, the chairman of what was ambitiously called our "Industrial Committee," rose to civic leadership after an early life as a country grocer and then a car salesman. When we met, he was sixty-five and ran a small loan office (but the paper called him "a financier," not a loan shark). To the displeasure of some who revered our earlier history as an "outpost" of culture and civilization on the early nineteenth-century frontier, he was cobbling together a ramshackle shopping center from the remnants of what had been Bethel College.

Marvin never went to college, but with only a high school education, he had become modestly affluent and had acquired a certain polish over the years. He had a practiced smiling charm that eased his entrepreneurial ventures into the boardrooms of northern companies in *Fortune* magazine's top 500. Beginning with a postcard survey of the dairy cows in Logan County—he wrote all the farmers to count how many—this became the census that persuaded the Kraft company to build a cheese plant in Russellville. Then, when Colonel Willard Rockwell of Pittsburgh dropped by on a search for a site for a die casting plant, Mr. Stuart showed him Elmer Shelton's cornfield, newly optioned to the chamber of commerce, on the road to Hopkinsville.

"How much do you want for this field?" Rockwell asked.

"One dollar, and it's yours," said Stuart with a twinkle in his eye.

To his credit, Rockwell paid a fair price, in 1954, and then gave us a gruff, crusty but big-hearted plant manager, Harry Whipple, a former Pennsylvania farm boy who spoke our language. Harry always conferred with Stuart on whom to hire (to make sure they wouldn't sign a union card) and enthusiastically recommended Logan County to every industrial prospect Stuart brought his way for the next fifteen years.

When Marvin took a small delegation from the chamber to visit a big midwest company, one wit in the group was awed by his salesmanship. He reported back to me that the old man pleaded with the company CEO "not to spoil our folks at the start" by overpaying them. "We are a simple people who enjoy the rural life—hunting and fishing, watching high school games on Friday nights and eating dinner on the grounds after Sunday church services," Stuart told the CEO. He wasn't even finished with this pitch, my informant said, when the CEO exclaimed, "Gimme that pen!" and signed a contract.

The owner of the Kaintuck Hotel where I lived when I was trying to kick booze said that in his first year in Russellville, when he walked downtown for breakfast at the Parkview on the Square, he would meet Marvin coming home for lunch. Maybe an exaggeration, but this was another almost believable story about an admired leader who created over 2,000 new industrial jobs in our farm community and found a way to keep many of our children at home.

*Chapter 4*

# Jobs: Doc Beauchamp Calls Frankfort

*May 5, 2005*

When I was a country editor in Kentucky fifty years ago, to get a state job of any kind you talked to a local politician who had friends in Frankfort.

Beginning in 1960, the new Merit System was supposed to emphasize, well, *merit.*

But when my friend Tom, the young Presbyterian minister in Russellville, was engaged to Joan, who had a Merit job as a social worker in Mayfield, I went to the Logan County political boss Emerson "Doc" Beauchamp to secure Joan's transfer to our area.

Lawrence W. Wetherby (left), Kentucky governor (1950–1955), and his lieutenant governor, Emerson "Doc" Beauchamp of Logan County, loved a good time, as when they joined in song, seen here, but they are credited with a solid administration between those of Governors Earle C. Clements and A.B. "Happy" Chandler in his second term. *Courtesy of Logan County Public Library.*

Beauchamp quickly dialed a Frankfort number from his home, but, while waiting on the line, he had a last minute question: "Say, Al, she IS a Democrat, ain't she?"

Beauchamp was a kingmaker of governors and less whose second home was Frankfort. When he died in 1971, Congressman Frank Albert Stubblefield asked me to help him secure the Beauchamp papers for Murray State University. But there were no papers. Doc did it all on the telephone.

# Part II
## *Crossing the County Line*

## *Chapter 5*

# I Become a Capitalist

Redirecting myself to a life without liquor, I spent a sober year testing my resolve, then bought a 10 percent interest in the *News-Democrat* from the Evans family owners who had put up with my struggles the first five years in the county. They and I were correct in the assumption that I would stay sober, but the elderly widowed publisher and I fell out five years later when she refused my offer to buy the remaining 90 percent of the paper.

Frustrated by her refusal and discouraged because her three children were pursuing lives away from Kentucky and leaving me to cope with their mother's indecisions about the future, I had organized a group of local investors who then approved a switch in plans. We started a rival paper, the *Logan Leader* in May 1968. After three months, the competition ended when my embittered former publisher sold to us and left the state. It was a rewarding but painful victory. Well aware that she tolerated me when few other employers might have, then took me in as a minority partner, I still regret that we could not reach an agreement without a mini-war over control of the paper. A history of the county reports that I unfailingly credited her with sheltering me in my bad times and more. Still, the public acceptance of the new ownership never convinced me that an amicable transition would not have been better.

While a terrible and unnecessary war raged in Vietnam, the sixties and seventies were go-go years of mergers and expansions in business. Between 1968 and 1976, my company acquired four other county seat papers in the region, amassing debt but also enough revenue to build a central printing

As editor turned publisher in Russellville, and with the help of local investors, I built a central printing plant in Russellville and acquired several other weeklies in the region, then started a suburban weekly near Nashville. Our plant, built to house a modern press, background left, with proud proprietor, won several architectural awards for adaptation of a historic building downtown. *Courtesy Smith family, Photo by Robert K. Stuart.*

plant downtown and then start a suburban weekly near Nashville. Enamored of the chase, I became skilled at negotiating buyouts. In one town, I closed the deal by hiring the seller's wife as editor. At a county with a state park, I promised the lady owner, a religious "dry," that I would never support legal liquor in a local option election. Then there was the owner who sold to me over a better offer because the rival owned more papers than I did and, disliking all chains, he preferred my little group as the lesser of two evils.

Other than printing my newly purchased papers on a modern offset press in Russellville and hiring a few bright young people as editors when I could get them, I can't claim I improved their content as much as I would have liked. My attention distracted by business concerns, I wrote less while I chased the numbers. Going into business, first in Russellville to "save my own voice" as an owner, then focusing on buying other papers, I almost lost it. Republican governor Louie Nunn jokingly asked me, "How does the Yellow Dog Democrat owner of a Democrat rag in Russellville publish the God-fearing *Green River Republican* in Morgantown in Butler County?"

"Very damn cautiously," I responded. "I seldom show my face over there."

In Russellville, my close friend, the attorney Granville Clark, shook his head one day over lunch after his mother, a fiery leader for historic preservation, scolded me for not strongly editorializing against a new courthouse.

"Smith, you are not the gutsy editor you used to be," he said. "You are just another capitalist."

*Chapter 6*

# Checks from LBJ

In 1963, our paper endorsed Edward T. "Ned" Breathitt Jr. of Hopkinsville for governor. Then only thirty-eight, Breathitt, an attorney, defeated the better-known A.B. "Happy" Chandler in the Democratic primary. A surprise pick by the incumbent governor, Bert T. Combs, to protect a new sales tax, which had fueled Combs' legacy of progressive legislation, Breathitt beat the early odds and defeated Chandler by a landslide. The general election, in which Chandler supported the Republican nominee, was much closer, but Breathitt won over Louie Nunn of Glasgow by thirteen thousand votes.

Inaugurated shortly after President John F. Kennedy was assassinated on November 22, Breathitt was winding up his first month in office when he had an unexpected visitor in late afternoon of New Year's Eve. It was the veteran mountain congressman Carl D. Perkins, who suggested they call the new president, Lyndon B. Johnson.

The rough-hewn Perkins was a powerful figure in Washington, chairman of the House Committee on Education and Labor, but a startled Breathitt, who had never met Johnson, objected that the president and his family were at their Texas ranch for the holiday. Perkins was unfazed and personally dialed the ranch number on the governor's desk phone. As Breathitt and his press secretary Don Mills, who was present, recalled to me years later, Perkins identified himself to someone who answered the call and asked to speak "to Lyndon."

An amazed Breathitt gasped when Johnson came on the line. "Mr. President," said Perkins, "Happy New Year. You have a pencil? Well, about that new courthouse for Hazard…" and went on with a request for favors while LBJ scribbled them down. The bold call ended with Perkins introducing the astonished young governor and handing the phone to Breathitt, who wished the new president success as the most powerful politician on the planet.

This was the beginning of a long relationship between Breathitt and the Johnson administration. When LBJ visited the troops at Fort Campbell in 1964, he joined Breathitt for a helicopter flyover in Western Kentucky, pledging to fully fund the 170,000 acres that had been set aside as the Land Between the Lakes. The president also agreed to fund 50 percent of what became Barkley State Park at a cost of $9 million

The tragedy of Johnson's failures with the Vietnam War and his conflicted personality as what a historian called a "flawed giant" have never persuaded me that he was not a great or near great president. The country desperately needed his victories for Civil Rights. Elements of his campaign for a Great Society and against poverty—for education and health care, the arts and the environment, a more secure safety net, and improved infrastructure—shame, by comparison, much of the record of many national leaders who followed.

From LBJ's programs, our papers promoted opportunities that began with Great Society checks from Washington. Russellville and Logan County leaders wrangled extra funds for new schools, a regional library, medical services, water and sewer lines, sanitary garbage collections, parks and recreation and concerts and theatrical programs of artistic merit. We boosted these improvements to "sell" our community to new industries.

A "cause" journalist, always chasing projects, I was stretched thin in my little publishing company —undercapitalized and never developing to full potential the papers I bought. But I was too ambitious to reject invitations to serve on, and in several cases lead, state associations supporting the press, the arts and education and economic development. Considering my troubled youth, the recognition was gratifying, but probably at a cost to the business bottom line.

Despite my deprecating reflections, there were talented employees and loyal stockholders who advanced our company, especially after I began working in broadcast journalism in 1974. To host and produce a weekly program called *Comment on Kentucky*, I was hired by the new Kentucky Educational Television network (KET), funded by another of LBJ's innovations, the Corporation for Public Broadcasting. Len Press, the founding director of KET, courageously gave me the freedom and a budget to hire top journalists for an uncensored discussion of issues in the news.

On a visit to highlight his War on Poverty, President and Mrs. Lyndon B. Johnson leave a cabin in Martin County in Appalachian Eastern Kentucky. Governor Edward T. Breathitt follows them down the path. *Courtesy of the Associated Press.*

I was on the air for over three decades, excepting time out as federal co-chairman in Washington of the Appalachian Regional Commission. The ARC was another legacy of the LBJ era. Spending millions on roads and other services for economic development in thirteen states, the ARC began with high hopes but along the way acquired critics for some of its policies and grants. While admitting its disappointments, I never found many citizens in the region who wanted to give back a foot of water pipe or sewer line, a mile of road, a bridge, airport or hospital. There were frustrations and tensions, but when I resigned after serving both Presidents Carter and Reagan, our company had borrowed a lot of money to buy the *Sentinel-Echo* in London in Laurel County in Appalachian Kentucky. This was the state's largest weekly. When Martha Helen and I moved there with our younger daughter to manage the new paper, we had committed our personal resources to a region that was called "distressed," but where we believed our prospects were good in an increasingly vibrant community. We were not disappointed.

# Part III
# *Appalachia*

## *Chapter 7*

# Mountain Journalist

On Inauguration Day for Ronald Reagan, Martha Helen and I drove out to Andrews Air Force Base to wave a morose goodbye to our departing leader Jimmy Carter. By May 1981, we had bought the new paper and moved to London, Democrats in traditionally Republican Laurel County.

With flat land at the edge of the mountains, seventy-five miles south of Lexington on I-75, Laurel County glittered with federal "gold": water and sewer lines, ARC roads, agency services for forestry and mining regulations, a U.S. Courthouse and an airport large enough to land Republican presidents on Air Force One. Our first week there, an FBI agent told me he spent most of his time on white collar crime and public corruption, largely in the mountain counties to the east. Editor Charles House disabused me of illusions about our new home. "You just think you are in East Kentucky," he said. "But go over to my hometown of Manchester in Clay County—now that's *serious* Appalachia!"

When Ronald Reagan's interior secretary James Watt, a right-winger and controversial from the start, discovered on a visit to London our first month that I was still in my ARC job as a Jimmy Carter holdover, he grimaced. "We will see about *that,*" he said menacingly. But he didn't see anything of the kind. I politely quit three times before Reagan accepted my resignation nineteen months after Watt's threat. A warm letter of praise from the president was framed and hung under a small spotlight behind my desk to disconcert Laurel County Republican leaders who couldn't get over a Democrat owning their paper.

Assuring our readers that we were there to give them lively journalism, not change their politics, I got back to my opinionated self in print and crusaded for better hospitals and schools. With local people and a new ally, Fifth District Republican congressman Hal Rogers of Somerset, we enlisted regional newspaper editors and organized a campaign for school improvements called "Forward in the Fifth."

A new citizens committee we supported proposed replacing a small Catholic hospital in London and a Baptist hospital in neighboring Corbin with one comprehensive modern full-service facility. We came close but failed when the Corbin hospital owners in Louisville moved a site application farther away from London and the London hospital owners in Lexington leased out their facility to a Texas corporation. Despite the religious cover, both hospitals were actually feeders to their larger facilities in Lexington. I was moved to tell our committee that, sadly, the greed of the Baptists was matched by the duplicity of the Catholics. In a fight over dollars, the goal was keeping the status quo, but the ruckus certainly boosted circulation, along with more letters to the editor, as we added an op-ed page and local columnists.

London's opportunities as a "growth center" for business (that flat land and good roads) attracted entrepreneurs like our new friend Ken James, who employed hundreds of people in data processing and supported his wife, Joanne's, leadership of Forward in the Fifth.

In a visit from the Ford Foundation's staff, I gave a glowing report on employment by food services—plants processing milk, bread and pies, and a large wholesale distributor, Laurel Grocery, operated for most of the century by two families, the Griffins and Chesnuts, who proved they could get along in the land of the feuding Hatfields and McCoys. It was also pleasing to note the success and large employment numbers of local road builders, especially the Greer family. Starting out as Greer Brothers with an outside partner, they built sections of I-75 and then split up. I told the Ford staffers, "Each of the three brothers owned his own contracting company, his own bank and his own Baptist Church!"

Four years later, with the Wal-Marting of small towns like those in which we published newspapers, I gave in and joined the sellout on Main Street of banks, real estate firms, hospitals, car dealers and media companies. Our company sold our papers to Park Communications of Ithaca, New York. Like new rich coal operators, Martha Helen and I sent our daughter Ginny to a New England boarding school and took the money and "ran" to Lexington. But I was haunted by the sorrowful comment of my friend Tom

Martha Helen Smith on a stroll with Al after moving to Lexington. In London, after earlier careers, she revitalized the business side of the paper and made it the most profitable of any in the company. She chaired the Appalachian Regional Healthcare for three years of her eighteen years as trustee. *Courtesy of* Lexington Herald-Leader.

Gish, who did not sell his weekly *Mountain Eagle* in Whitesburg: "We are all Appalachians now." In a global economy, was that the work force of rural America—employees in branch plants for distant owners?

When we sold our weekly papers in the '80s, agriculture was changing in Logan County, with fewer small family farms. Land ownership went the way of so much of our economy, consolidated into fewer hands. Leslie Page III of Lexington and his brother Ben inherited a farm from their mother, Virginia, my partner in the newspapers, and their father, but they lease the land to neighbor Lee Robey. Les estimates that twenty-five to thirty families operate farms of more than two thousand acres in Logan County. Lee Robey and his children manage thirteen thousand to fourteen thousand acres, including the largest dairy in Kentucky. Billy Joe Miles of Owensboro, a former chairman of the board of trustees at the University of Kentucky, with many agri-business interests, may own as much as six thousand acres in Logan County. Some say he is the largest landowner in Kentucky. Maybe not exactly corporatized, but many "family" farms are now mega-business!

*Chapter 8*

# Beauty and Tragedy

## A review of *A History of Appalachia* by Richard B. Drake

*March 11, 2000*

In this new social history, beginning with the often-misunderstood Indian era and ending with Bill Clinton's problematic welfare reform, the reader will find, in fewer than three hundred pages, a remarkably comprehensive single-volume account of Appalachia—the plain but plucky folks who cleared its forests, mined its coal and fought its wars, the plutocrats who exploited its rich resources and the ruined hopes of ordinary men and women who struggled for justice.

The author, Richard B. Drake, a retired history professor at Berea College, gives as fair a treatment as I have seen, in a short space, of the troublesome issues that plague a people who have been stereotyped over the years as peculiar, set apart and unskilled at coping with the challenges of work, school, health and creating civil and prosperous communities.

This book from University Press of Kentucky acknowledges that any inclusive picture of this region must admit the other world of Main Street successes by local entrepreneurs, schools that challenge their students, improved health services and a network of improved roads and infrastructure to promote towns that the government labels growth centers. (Indeed, many Appalachian schoolchildren now score as well on tests as poor kids in non-Appalachian Kentucky.) That said, Drake notes that, beginning with early studies of the region in the 1900s by liberal churchmen, "most of Appalachian scholarship betrays a strong anger against American corporate capitalism…

The sheer ferocity and magnitude of this radical Appalachian scholarship attests to the kind of tragic picture that Appalachian history presents."

Here, the Kentucky reader who is too pressed for time to ponder Drake's list of outrages has a simple option: just recall the headlines in recent newspapers, those that bannered the collapse of a coal impoundment that fouled miles of streams; mining boards that don't punish violators; black-lung benefits that are denied; trash cleanup laws that are weakened; and big cash donations to politicians from coal magnates who want exemptions from clean-air laws.

While not yet as fateful as the Buffalo Creek disaster in West Virginia in February 1972, where hundreds perished and a whole valley was wiped out when a gob pile dam burst, the current Kentucky problems with regulating public safety and the environment in the mountains are different only in degree. They fester in a society so indifferent to its history that the smallest measures to reverse its own destruction—truck weight laws or enforcing dust testing in the mines—are acclaimed as milestones of progress.

One of Drake's interesting "rusties" (a folk term for "riddles") is whether Appalachia is a place or a state of mind. Congress mandated the Appalachian Regional Commission (ARC) to define the territory, for purposes of investing tax dollars, as including all of West Virginia and parts of twelve other states, including forty-nine counties in Kentucky.

The venerable James Still, however, long ago described Appalachia as "a somewhat mythical region," then added, "but the heart of it is in Eastern Kentucky." Still, who has lived around Troublesome Creek and Hindman for nearly seventy years, is the author of the twentieth-century classic *River of Earth,* a novel about a coal-field family in transition. Drake, who began teaching Berea's first Appalachian Studies courses in 1959, writes that "the region did not develop its own clear and strong literary voice until the 1930s" with the appearance of Still and Jesse Stuart, James Agee, Thomas Wolfe and, later, Harriette Simpson Arnow, who "has written what is probably the region's epic novel, *The Dollmaker.*"

So what is Appalachia? Drake summarizes the familiar negatives: a mineral and timber colony exploited for absentee owners; a failed experiment by successive waves of missionaries (church, school and government) imposing their agendas; and a land of gun-toting, violence-prone boobs and zealots, an anti-intellectual people who worship with snakes in the midst of welfare-dependency.

And positives: Appalachia represents "the best of traditional America, keeper of the nation's historic individualism, its self-sufficiency, and self-

A modest log cabin provided warmth and shelter for a mountain family. *Courtesy of University of Kentucky, postcard collection.*

sacrifice." It is a haven from the grasping materialism of the cities, a chance to live in harmony with nature's rhythms.

As the stereotypes reinforce or collide with each other, Drake deftly moves on to other ideas. He offers his own conviction that "Appalachia represents a significant and distinct region within the larger American society."

The historic evidence "of the overwhelmingly rural society that existed before 1930, with a sense of separateness" is one of five basic interpretations that influence his book. A second theme is "the emergence of a regional economy largely dependent upon outside sources of cash, and the concomitant loss of economic control of the region's resources as development took place."

Another idea stresses the persistence of what he terms a "yeomanesque mentality" or attitude—land to be farmed, seen as a resource for the family, "not a commodity to be bought or sold." Two more themes touch on "the strong and continuing presence of wilderness" and an admission that Appalachia is so complex, vast and varied "that practically any point of view may find some verification."

Drake applauds Wendell Berry for teaching that farming in reverence for the land is a religious act. In the recent theories about Appalachia's future, Drake sees a connection between Berry and Mahatma Gandhi, who preached a kind of sustainable economy that recognized that modernization may not be desirable in all occasions.

Although I never met any Eastern Kentuckians who called themselves "Appalachians" instead of Pike or Bell Countians, or wherever was home, the scholars claim they know who is who in the hills. Cratis Williams, "the Dean of Appalachian studies," grouped the folks into town elites, substantial farmers and "Branchwater Mountaineers." Charles Smith, a professor at Cumberland College, said they were "town folk," "hollow folk" and "big road folk"—essentially "hollow folk on their way to town." Loyal Jones of Berea College says that Appalachian religion is the key that unlocks mountain culture. He says the idea of people being cursed by "original sin" enables them not to be astonished at evil and to overcome adversity by enduring it.

Harry Caudill, the most influential Appalachian of my lifetime, claimed there are just two kinds of people in the region: the rich and the powerful who dominate everybody else, and everybody else, mostly poor and powerless.

But in 1988, when the civic activists led by Kentuckians for the Commonwealth won passage of the constitutional amendment repealing the pernicious broad form deed, Caudill wrote a celebratory letter to his fellow Appalachian, former governor Bert Combs.

In the letter, Combs told me at the time, "He writes that he and I have lived long enough to see the end of the dominance of Big Coal."

"What do you think?" I asked Combs. "I wrote him back and said, 'I doubt it,'" Combs replied.

Since 2001, of course, we have witnessed the deaths of twenty-nine miners at the Upper Big Branch Mine in April 2010, while the coal industry and its minions continue the "war" on the EPA and the Obama administration. Renewed "coal wars" in central Appalachia between the mining industry and environmentalists focus on mountain top removal—the need to mine coal versus the damage to the land. The recent emergence of gas production in northern Appalachia brings controversies over "fracking," the process of forcing pressurized fluids deep into rock to crack it, releasing gas. Many fear gas leaking into groundwater.

Evidence from medical scientists cites the linkage between coal production and poor health. Cancer rates are 50 percent higher and kidney disease rates 70 percent higher in residents living closer to surface mining, according to the Rural Health Research Center at West Virginia University, recently reported in the *Lexington Herald-Leader*. New attention to dental health followed the Diane Sawyer documentary on poor dental health in children of Appalachia, but the show raised old issues of stereotyping by outsiders. Eastern Kentucky has experienced a huge rise of prescription drug abuse reflecting greater social anxiety, unhappiness and depression, as measured by multiple surveys.

Finally, my friend and UK historian Ron Eller, perhaps the foremost academic authority on Appalachia, notes that we have witnessed the continued expansion of the number of counties that are part of the ARC, but we have seen little change in the level of funding for the agency or any national interest in fighting poverty.

Eller, author of a brilliant study of Appalachia since 1945, *Uneven Ground*, University Press of Kentucky, 2008, argues that if there is anything new in the scholarship since 2000 it is a greater focus on the issues in Appalachia as part of national cultural and political challenges, rather than just as Appalachian problems—think energy and global warming, corporate plutocracy and power, declining democracy and the culture of consumption.

There is a growing recognition, says Eller, in a letter to me, "that the problems of Appalachia are the problems of America as Harry [Caudill, the lawyer activist of the mountains] argued as well. The Appalachian history is deeply connected to the national story, not separate from it, as we once argued about the region."

My own efforts have focused on rural America in general, as well as Appalachia, through the Institute for Rural Journalism and Community Issues at University of Kentucky, which I co-founded, now directed by my longtime journalism colleague Al Cross. It focuses on four issues: education, health, the environment and economic development.

## Chapter 9

# Generations: An American Family by John Egerton

## Twentieth Anniversary Edition 2003

*Reviewed in Fall 2003*

In 1983, as John Egerton's research and writing journey down the trail of the Ledford family's two and a half centuries in America was closing between the covers of this fine book, word came that Burnam Ledford, who was 106, was finally dying at the Garrard County hospital in Lancaster. The old man was ready to go, but he wanted to see Egerton one more time.

As Egerton placed the typed page proofs in his lap, Burnam Ledford said, "I've always told you I'd try to wait around until you come back," but he only glanced at the first paragraphs. A week later, four generations of Ledfords gathered to bury the hero of the book at the Paint Lick Cemetery at Manse in Garrard County.

When they gathered again, in December 1987, to bury Burnam's beloved wife, Addie, she had died six weeks shy of her 103rd birthday. Asked by the family to "say a few words," Egerton found himself choked with emotion. *Generations*, published the year of Burnam's death, had won the prestigious Weatherford Award for writing about Appalachia and had been acclaimed as one of the country's two hundred best books of the year. Now with Addie's passing, he knew that the long winding story of the Ledfords as told to him by Burnam and Addie "had finally reached an end."

The story covers the Ledfords' recollections of Harlan County in the eastern Kentucky mountains and of what happened when Burnam's parents pulled up stakes to escape the feuds in Harlan and traveled 135 miles northwest by ox-drawn covered wagons to a new start in the knobby hills of Garrard County.

An exemplary work of oral history, *Generations* was crafted from six years of interviews and research into letters, courthouse records, charts and photographs. In Egerton's hands, the Ledfords' story "becomes a small American epic," a *Washington Post* reviewer wrote in 1983. The new edition, with intriguing family pictures, revisits and updates the Ledford clan, concluding that a reunion this year in Lexington or Harlan would draw 144 direct descendants from the 1903 marriage of Burnam and Addie King.

The late Cawood Ledford, the famed UK sports broadcaster who was born and died in Harlan County, was a distant cousin of Burnam Ledford. Most of the Ledfords in America are descended from three brothers who came from England to Virginia and then to North Carolina in 1738, Egerton says.

Egerton, of Nashville, who has also written about the civil rights struggle in the South and southern food, grew up in Cadiz, Kentucky, and attended Western Kentucky University and the University of Kentucky. He was already a successful author when he began the search in 1977 for a family whose generational and personal stories might provide a representative social history of America. He had combed through a dozen states when a newspaper story about the Ledfords' longevity took him to Lancaster.

Burnam had been a farmer, a hardware store manager and a lifelong supporter of the Republican Party. Addie was the daughter of a Harlan County sheriff and farmer and grew up in a home with amenities that included a pump organ and a subscription to the *New York Tribune*. Each had briefly taught school, when an eighth-grade education would qualify for the job.

"History lived in them," Egerton writes. "In the year of Burnam's birth, the United States celebrated its first century as a nation. Alexander Graham Bell introduced the telephone. Mark Twain published *The Adventures of Tom Sawyer* and General George Custer died at the Battle of Little Big Horn. On the day before Burnam and Addie were married, Orville and Wilbur Wright launched their fragile airplane at Kitty Hawk, North Carolina."

Of their thirteen children, ten had lived to become adults, but only one, a daughter, Gwen Gastineau, had remained in Garrard (pronounced "Garrit") County. Despite their great age, Egerton found them to be intellectually alert

Burnam and Addie King Ledford on their seventy-ninth anniversary, December 18, 1982. They had 144 direct descendants when author John Egerton took this picture for his prize-winning book. *Courtesy of John Egerton.*

and informed on national events, with memories certain as the ring of a mountain farm bell.

Burnam was five years old when he was taken to see his great-grandmother on Crank's Creek in Harlan. "She was born in 1781 when George Washington was president," he told Egerton. "She was Aley's Betsy, the widow of Aley Ledford, the man that brought our family name into Kentucky" in 1808.

Aley (for "Alexander") Ledford, who freed the Sinkler (originally "St. Clair") family of slaves who came with him through the Cumberland Gap and left them eight hundred acres of land, was a successful settler, but when Egerton took Burnam, the centenarian, back one more time to Harlan County, not one of Aley's eighty-six thousand acres remained in their family, and much of the land on Martin's Fork and Crank's Creek was so torn by strip mining that Burnam told Cawood Ledford's father, Wash Ledford, he couldn't recognize anything.

*Generations* has been a best seller for University Press of Kentucky. This anniversary edition invites a new audience to the pleasures of local and regional history as interpreted by a master journalist through the voices of those who lived it.

"Every family has a story to tell," Egerton writes, "but only the most fortunate has resident story tellers to nourish the roots and keep the chronicle alive. Without them—without such people as Burnam and Addie to breathe air and light into the murky past—we are like miners without lamps, digging in the dark."

## *Chapter 10*

# "A Beggar for Paupers"

*April 30, 2003*

Science having just finished mapping the human genome, is it churlish to lament a less enlightened era when we didn't know as much about the body's DNA, but the voters were more up close and personal with the body politic?

While bioscience is making progress, can we say the same of political science? In the governor's race, what's to like in any of those TV attack ads from cyber space? How do we cheer or cry over a news report about a court order ousting a candidate we never knew in the first place?

In the Russellville weekly paper, my successor as editor, Jim Turner, complains that live in-person candidates are dissing Logan County—seldom seen in a courthouse where the Rhea-Beauchamp gang could once deliver a dependable 2,000 Democratic votes to make or break a state race.

No need, then, to ask how long has it been since a chartered bus plastered with Republican banners paused in Tompkinsville for pastoral encouragement of the Carter family's Monroe County faithful?

Lost to paid TV and visits to targeted urban counties with big numbers for the major parties are the days when rural voters met the candidates in the flesh, not on cable, or KET. When a politician lied to you, he did it in your face while hugging the baby. You could smell the onions.

Jim Kelly, a Social Security director in the mountains, remembers when Congressman Carl D. Perkins skipped a speech at an overly long political rally in Pikeville but exhorted the crowd not to leave until he had individually spoken with everybody there. Seventy-five citizens filed through the door pumping Carl D.'s hand on the way out and telling him what he hadn't done for them lately.

Not exactly how we communicate today, but that's the way Mr. Perkins stayed in touch. One of the last of the New Deal liberals, he held enormous power in Washington, flowing from the poorest of the poor who kept him there until he controlled every federal dollar spent for education in the United States. "I'm just a beggar for paupers," he said. Quaint words, but they were from his heart, not from a ghost writer, and they resonated in every election until his heart gave out on an August day in 1984, flying home on the Piedmont to the hills of East Kentucky.

This Friday and Saturday as the mountain's movers and shakers hold their annual leadership conference at Hazard to worry over issues of poverty and image, the rest of us who are depressed by our sorry state of politics might think about what made Perkins such an effective champion of his Appalachian people. Looking for what few say they see or hear in the governor's race, but what was always found in Carl D., perhaps the answer is *connectedness.*

# Part IV

# *Storytellers and Poets*

*Chapter 11*

# A Feast of Age

*July 12, 1998*

*Some of the richest land in the United States is to be found in Bluegrass Kentucky. Like the huge oaks that spread their long sinewy arms far out from their great trunks, the land has stamina.*
—*Thomas D. Clark,* The Kentucky

*The stranger who had stopped at a filling station near Hindman for gas said to the attendant, "I'm from out of state. I'm down here looking around for Appalachia. Where do you think Appalachia is?" The attendant answered, "Appalachia is over in Virginia. It's a town." And the stranger said, "No, no. I mean the area they call Appalachia." To this the attendant said, "I don't know myself, but if you'll go on down the road to the next station there's a fellow who'll tell you. He don't know either, but he'll tell you something."*
—*James Still,* The Wolfpen Notebooks

Widely respected for what they each in their long lives have learned and so movingly written about Kentucky, its land and its people, historian and civic activist Thomas D. Clark of Lexington and mountain poet and storyteller James Still of Hindman will celebrate birthdays this week. Clark will be ninety-five on Tuesday, and Still will be ninety-two on Thursday.

And yes, they're going strong. After they appeared together with *Courier-Journal* editorial director and vice-president David Hawpe on KET's *Comment*

Historian Thomas D. Clark and poet and storyteller James Still came to Kentucky as outsiders but stayed on to become revered citizens. They were in their nineties when sharing this meal together. *Courtesy of Warren Brunner, Berea, Kentucky.*

*on Kentucky*, the ninety-six-year-old father of my friend Guy Richardson, a Danville grocer, told his son, "Those old boys are holding up well, a lot sharper than those reporter fellows."

There will be a cake and candles for Clark at next weekend's meeting of the Prichard Committee for Academic Excellence at Lake Cumberland State Park. Honoring Still, the Hindman Settlement School has sent out seven hundred invitations to share cake and ice cream next Saturday at his century-old log house on Little Carr Creek between Wolfpen Creek and Dead Mare Branch.

For nearly seventy years, Clark has been involved with education as a University of Kentucky history professor and department head, as author of some two dozen books about the state and the South and as a crusader for better schools, libraries and other programs to support them.

Michael Adams, former Centre College president and now head of the University of Georgia, calls him "Kentucky's most distinguished citizen." Former governor Edward T. Breathitt, who was one of the twenty-five thousand students Clark estimates he taught at UK, says he is "a state treasure."

The published body of Still's literary work is not large—a novel, a dozen or so short stories, less than one hundred poems in three collections, a notebook of "sayings" and some work for children: nursery rhymes, tales and riddles. Not large—thirteen slender books—but the reputation grows. The novel *River of Earth*, published in 1940, is called an American classic, compared favorably with John Steinbeck's *The Grapes of Wrath*, published within the same year. The short stories—narrated, as was the novel, by a boy in the coal camps—remind critics of similar perspectives in fiction by Twain, Hemingway and Faulkner. For his poems, Still was acclaimed by the late James Dickey, author of *Deliverance*, as "the truest and most remarkable poet that the mountain culture has produced."

For all their reputation, why are these men such enduring figures of respect in Kentucky? Why the birthday publicity and standing ovations? James Still says that for perhaps half of the more than sixty years he has lived in Knott County, he never met a neighbor who had read anything he wrote. Clark's *History of Kentucky*, first published in 1937, has given way (with his encouragement) to James Klotter and Lowell Harrison's *New History of Kentucky*. How many Kentucky legislators who named Clark the state's historian laureate and Still its poet laureate ever opened one of their books?

The answer isn't complicated. They are gifted and talented at what they do, and they have been at it a long time. Their life work shows how much they love us, despite our faults. And we love them back, often at second-hand remove, because we have simply *heard* about what they wrote or said or did.

In the vernacular of Still's mountain folks, both are "fotched on" men. They came here as outsiders—Clark from Mississippi and Still from Alabama—and became insightful insiders. Although he wasn't a hermit ("I need people, and I need a few of them to need me"), Still's choice of a home in the isolated mountains created an unrivaled authenticity for his stories and poems about "the machine in the garden," the impact of industrialization on Eastern Kentucky.

The more extroverted Clark, on the other hand, put down his roots in the bluegrass to cultivate a career as the foremost scholar of the commonwealth's history. Clark was a friend of William Faulkner when the future Nobel Prize–winning novelist was scratching out early stories as a student dropout at Ole Miss. The historian came to UK for one degree in 1928 ("and saw my first Republican"). Four years later, with a doctorate from Duke, he returned to Kentucky to teach and start the special collections project at the UK library.

Still's first and enduring Kentucky base was a different school. In the Depression, Hindman Settlement couldn't pay him a salary, but they offered room and board if the young vacation bible school and youth worker from Alabama would stay as librarian. "With three degrees, no job and no prospects, I was at the jumping-off place." But he also knew, he says, "that I was where I wanted to be, that these mountains were home." In 1936, when he decided to leave the settlement school and write full time, he was finally earning about fifteen dollars a month. "For six years' labor, I earned six cents a day."

But he also published his first book of poetry, and it was now time to move to that log house and complete his novel, *River of Earth.* Some ten miles from Hindman, over a rutted wagon road and up a creek bed, "I knew why I had come there, but some of the neighbors were less sure." They called him "the man in the bushes," and one said, "He's quit a good job [the fifteen dollars a month] and come over in here and sot down."

In Lexington, meanwhile, Clark was starting a family, writing books at night, teaching a full class load and trying to save historic Kentucky papers from destruction. The first break came with a report that truckloads of precious archival material were being hauled away from Frankfort warehouses to be sold for scrap. "I called Governor Chandler. He told me to tell the truck driver to stop it, to bring back the loads he had hauled to Louisville, and if he didn't he would be in the penitentiary by sundown," Clark remembers.

Although Clark retired from UK thirty years ago, President Charles Wethington says many Kentuckians think he's still teaching, so extraordinary and ongoing have been his crusades—for the new state library, the new state history center and the University Press projects, including the *Encyclopedia of Kentucky,* the *Atlas of Kentucky* and the *Encyclopedia of Louisville.*

Having lived almost half of the two centuries in which Kentucky has existed as a state, Clark exhorts young Kentuckians to "shun the traps of the past." Although he and his friend Still have both been string-savers of history, teasing out the threads that run through the warp and woof of our past, Clark says our leaders have been too enthralled in the name of conservatism to old-fashioned ideas of government that poorly served us. "Keep your eye on the twenty-first century" is his motto.

There are kind words for progress made, but in the summing up, these venerable and valuable citizens scorn what Clark calls "the careless waste of our natural resources."

Thinking of a time they both knew was kinder, less threatening to black and white warblers teetered along the banks of Dead Mare Branch, to minnows riffled in the summer pools, partridges calling in the water meadow and "a pair of rabbits flashed tails among the bluing weeds," Still confronts us in a poem, "Death of a Fox":

*Last night I ran a fox over.*
*A sudden brilliant flash of gold,*
*A setting sun of gilded fur*
*Appeared in my car's beam,*
*And then the fatal thump.*
*I asked the fox to forgive me.*
*He spat as he died.*
*I asked God to forgive me.*
*I don't believe He will.*
*Is there no pardon anywhere?*

Early on a snowy day in January in the 1990s, I picked up Dr. Clark about 6:00 a.m. for a mission to Frankfort. He was standing in a puddle of wet snow in front of his house in Lexington, and I thought, "My God, if old age doesn't get him, the weather will." But, when we drove up to the governor's mansion in Frankfort, he was chatting away about Kentucky politics as First Lady Libby Jones came out and joined us in my wife's Explorer. A few minutes later, we were in a secluded room in the Capitol annex basement with the leaders of the legislature.

Mrs. Jones and the venerable historian made eloquent appeals for the construction of a new history center. The request granted by the legislature, funded with public and private funds and started in the administration of Governor Brereton C. Jones, led to the $129 million 167,000-square-foot facility, dedicated in April 1999 in the presence of Dr. Clark. The center was renamed the Thomas D. Clark Center for Kentucky History shortly after his death June 28, 2005, at age 101.

*Chapter 12*

# A Laureate of Letters

## A review of *Robert Penn Warren: A Biography* by Joseph Blotner

*November 16, 1997*

Although Robert Penn Warren spent nearly all of his long, productive life away from Kentucky, and his best-known book, the novel *All the King's Men*, is set in Huey Long's Louisiana, no one disputes Kentucky's claim to Warren as its most distinguished author ever. Few critics will disagree with Warren's biographer, Joseph Blotner, that Warren was "America's pre-eminent man of letters."

A prodigious writer, with fifty-some volumes to his name, Warren's achievements as a poet, novelist, essayist, critic, editor, biographer, historian and professor of English are fully examined in Blotner's new biography. This country's first official poet laureate, Warren won the Pulitzer Prize for *All the King's Men* and two more Pulitzers for poetry—one a book of new poems, *Now and Then*, that came out in 1979 when he was seventy-four years old. The biographer in search of conflict to hold his reader turns to the personal.

Warren did contend with physical and emotional problems—he lost an eye in an accident. Divorced from his first wife after twenty years of marriage, there was a happy second marriage to the writer Eleanor Clark, and children—all in all, rather mild happenings compared to the difficulties of some writers, especially when success came so early in a career.

America's first poet laureate, Kentucky-born Robert Penn Warren, had a happy second marriage and two children with his second wife, the writer Eleanor Clark, seen at their home in Connecticut. *Courtesy of UK Special Collections.*

For Kentuckians and all serious readers, I think, the compelling interest is in how Warren grew from his rural Kentucky childhood in Todd County, on the Tennessee border near Nashville, to become a national figure of moral authority and artistic respect. There are arguments that no one much reads Warren's novels today.

Giving a little on this point while remembering that *All the King's Men* sold over three million copies, there is still no question that this man was a cultural force and a social hero. Blotner does an excellent job of telling us why.

Blotner's study of Mississippi's Faulkner was a useful preparation for Kentucky's Warren. Like Faulkner, Warren considered himself a modern Southern writer who admired contemporaries of the avant-garde—Eliot, Yeats and Hardy in poetry, and two novelists, Theodore Dreiser and Faulkner himself. Like Faulkner, Warren was profoundly marked by and forever confronting the traumas of his nineteenth-century forebears, slavery and the Civil War.

What Warren called his own "long hassle with the South" eventually produced seven books—five of them non-fiction—about slavery, the Civil War and the struggle for civil rights for blacks. Although poetry, sixteen volumes with time out for ten novels, was central to Warren's work, his meditations on race and roots spread through everything he did.

So Blotner begins, properly, at the beginning, in Old Kentucky. There, with Warren's encouragement and active support, by an author who admits upfront that he came to see his subject as a "genuinely good man," he uncovers in boyhood experiences, and in family background, origins of Warren's philosophical and poetic vision.

Events of actual violence suggest an early conditioning for the melodramatic and lurid elements that Warren employed to background his adult themes. These themes are the search for self-knowledge, the nature of time, the quest for identity, the misuses of power and the passage from innocence into a corrupt world where the old verities do not sustain and the path out is unclear.

The Warrens were the "aristocrats" of Guthrie, the railroad town where Warren was born in 1905. His father, Robert Franklin Warren, was a banker-merchant who himself wrote poetry, read books and seldom attended church. (He paid his young son to read the Bible all the way through, then gave him Darwin's *Origin of the Species.*) His mother, Anna Ruth Penn, who had been a schoolteacher, doted on her red-haired baby, the first of three children and the one who got the most education when the money ran out.

A Confederate veteran grandfather, Gabriel Thomas Penn, recalled Civil War atrocities, including his decision to hang a gang of marauding bushwhackers. Decades later, these ancestors would haunt the poetry, along with others Warren remembered from a county where, when the Civil War erupted, five thousand slaves more or less coexisted with seven thousand whites. And where, two years before his birth, the troubled tobacco farmers put on hoods, mounted horses after dark and terrorized neighbors who wouldn't cooperate in a struggle against the tobacco companies. (It was called the Black Patch War, and Warren's vision of how it destroyed its leaders became his first major novel, *Night Riders.*)

Homicide was a fact of life in Guthrie. Kent Greenfield, Warren's best friend when they were teenagers, declared in later years, "You wouldn't believe the people in my lifetime that have been killed in this town. Shot up. Cut up. Doctors come in here and stay overnight and say they've seen more blood than they've ever seen in their life."

Greenfield, who taught young Red Warren to swim and to catch a baseball, went off from Kentucky to another kind of fame, as a pitcher for John McGraw's New York Giants. Under alcohol, he would crash, as Warren remembered him in a poem, "and no batter/could do what booze finally did:/just blow him off the mound."

But also in Todd County were people of gentility and faith, some of them farmers of means who prized learning and supported churches. The Merriwethers and Gordons, who had intermarried, were such, including a daughter, Caroline Gordon, an aspiring writer home from college in summer 1924, when Warren introduced her to his house guest, his brilliant Vanderbilt roommate, Allen Tate. The Tate-Gordon marriage eventually broke up, but the story that they made love that summer in a Todd County cemetery endures.

Beginning with Tate's description of young Warren as "the most gifted person I've ever known," Blotner relates how Warren, Tate, Gordon and other Vanderbilt friends—including John Crowe Ransom, Donald Davidson, Andrew Lytle and Merrill Moore—would become famous as literary intellectuals (more accepted nationally than by the Vanderbilt establishment) after gaining an early reputation as the Vanderbilt Fugitive Agrarians—Fugitives from the name of their poetry magazine, and Agrarians from their opposition to the impact of industrialization on Old South values.

In a Depression-era South, these poets and some historian friends hung together long enough to publish the 1930 book of twelve essays, *I'll Take My Stand*. It became a landmark tract against modernism, still read and still discussed. Later Warren repeatedly repudiated his essay on what was then called "the Negro question."

By the 1970s, literate Kentuckians so admired Red Warren that the Kentucky Oral History Commission initiated forty-four taped interviews that Blotner cites in his research. The University of Kentucky held a seventy-fifth birthday symposium in his honor, not long after Jimmy Carter bestowed a Presidential Medal. Western Kentucky University established a Warren Center, and both UK and Western received Warren papers and memorabilia. (Later, upon hearing that Western Kentucky admirers wanted to buy his homeplace in Guthrie and move it to WKU in Bowling Green, Warren's comment was "Jesus Christ!")

Despite failing health, Warren's last years were mellow as he and Eleanor enjoyed Rosanna and Gabriel, both artists, the children of their late marriage, and visits from friends, many of them talented and famous, who came to their home. Although his poems and novel musings frequently invoked religious imagery of guilt, redemption and the struggle for faith, he died an unbeliever in a hereafter.

At his funeral at a Vermont churchyard, friends read from two of his strongest poems, "Bearded Oaks" and "Grackles." Cleanth Brooks, also a Kentuckian who edited with Warren two of the century's most influential texts on poetry and fiction, read from the *Book of Common Prayer*. There was no clergyman to pray for the old poet; Brooks would do.

The mourners could remember how Warren recalled Grandpa Penn in "Old-Time Childhood in Kentucky." The boy, beginning to be aware of the tragic sense of "what life is," asks, "What do you do, things being like this?" The old man answers, "All you can."

## *Chapter 13*

# Bingham's "Best Writer"

*August 3, 2006*

He was of medium stature, but John Ed Pearce was one of those bright, sly, complex characters, like his friend Ed Prichard, who loom tall in tales of Kentucky politics, journalism and memorable personalities.

Barry Bingham Sr. often referred to John Ed as "the best writer I ever hired at the *Courier-Journal* and *Louisville Times*." And when the national press called on John Ed for an appreciation of Bingham at his death, they had the right fellow. Pearce admired Barry's literary sensibilities and liberal political sympathies, but he also relished the publisher's patrician style.

They saw most issues alike and appreciated many of the same people, yet as they grew older, it was disconcerting to their mutual friends when Pearce occasionally professed to be disenchanted with the rewards of working for the Binghams. Those rewards were envied by other journalists—top status on a newspaper ranked among the best, bylines and choice assignments on important stories, a respected voice in editorial decisions and freedom to disagree with owners who were not punitive.

Gifted with a quick mind, attractive features, high energy and a poet's talent for words, he charmed a lot of women and impressed many men. But the good humor with which he engaged the mining of stories and the entertainment of dinner companions only slightly masked a notion that life had not dealt all the cards owed him.

John Ed Pearce was an editorial writer and popular columnist for the *Courier-Journal* and, after retirement, the Lexington *Herald-Leader*. His book *Divide and Dissent: Kentucky Politics 1930–1963* benefited from an intimate friendship with Governors Combs and Breathitt and their adviser Edward Prichard. *Courtesy of the* Courier-Journal.

At a Leadership Kentucky conference, when Bingham Sr. introduced Pearce, the keynote speaker, as the finest pen in his tenure on the Louisville papers, Pearce shot his old boss a scornful smile and replied, "Barry, if I was all that good, why didn't you pay me more?" It was not one of his attractive moments.

It was said of John Ed, by younger reporters at the *Courier-Journal*, that he "never met a rich man he didn't like" but that was reading his personal frustrations over having no fortune of his own into his deftly crafted profiles of wealthy Kentuckians, like Garvice Kinkaid, or the barons of Bluegrass horsedom—W.T. (Bill) Young comes to mind—that seemed to shine in reflections of solid gold.

Enjoying the society of the rich and famous was a paradox of Pearce's personality. He was one of the last authentic liberals in Kentucky public life. In editorials he wrote for the *Courier-Journal* and, later, his *Herald-Leader* Sunday columns, he was an advocate of a federal government that champions the poor and oppressed, defies the special interests and taxes the well heeled.

More than any other Kentucky journalist, he criticized the failure of capitalism to sustain the checks and balances that democracy deserves. He didn't just fault the system; in withering paragraphs he castigated the offenders, whether against the economy, the educational system or the environment, from presidents to county jailers, by name, rank and serial number.

In local and state politics, few if any reporters were more familiar than Pearce with the colorful but sordid customs of our courthouses and city halls, the deal-making culture of our state capitol; few were more disillusioned, but none was as enduringly supportive of a scattering of political leaders, all Democrats, of course, as was Pearce. His heroes were two former governors, Bert Combs and Combs's protégé and successor Edward (Ned) Breathitt. He respected and enjoyed an off again, on again relationship with Earle Clements, another former governor. It was the burly Clements who picked up Pearce and angrily shook him over a story, but Albert "Happy" Chandler so resented Pearce's preference for Clements, he doubtless would have done worse, choked him into eternal silence, given a chance.

Chandler, who had a touchy relationship with the Bingham family and their papers, referred to John Ed as "that little SOB, Pearce," but Pearce consistently credited Chandler for a landmark reorganization of state government in his first term, 1935-39, and for the creation of the Albert Benjamin Chandler Medical Center at University of Kentucky in his second term, 1955-59. Chandler, Clements and Combs were the central figures in the valuable book John Ed wrote about Democratic Party factionalism, *Divide and Dissent, Kentucky Politics, 1930-1963.*

Naturally Chandler was rankled by Pearce's friendship with Ed Prichard, the Harvard-educated lawyer from Bourbon County, a disciple of Franklin D. Roosevelt and of Earle Clements who became the fabled counselor to Combs and Breathitt after his own ambitions collapsed in an election scandal. While Prichard and Pearce shared a belief that this country was saved in the Depression by FDR's expansive use of government, Chandler, who boasted he was "allergic" to public debt, was sufficiently conservative to earn Prichard's quip that he was "the leader of the Republican wing of the Kentucky Democratic party."

An article by Pearce in the *Courier-Journal* magazine about Prichard's struggle to recover from a prison sentence for stuffing a ballot box in 1948 paved the path for Prichard's late-life recognition as an influential voice for progressive government and improvement of the public schools. A co-recipient of a Pulitzer Prize awarded the *Courier-Journal* for crusades against environmental abuses by the coal industry, John Ed was proud of his role in improving the state parks as a member of a commission in the Combs administration. This was the sort of service disdained by a later generation of journalists as too close to politicians in power, but Pearce had the backing of the Binghams at the time. This was not the case, however, when Chandler embarrassed the paper by pointing out that Pearce and Combs became partners in a real estate investment in Florida, a venture that was quickly dissolved by demand of Barry Bingham Sr.

Ed Prichard was not the only beneficiary of Pearce's skill at turning a narrative of misfortune into a portrait of recovery. After a visit to my newspaper office in Russellville to write about change in small towns, John Ed transformed the assignment into an account of my battle with alcoholism on the New Orleans papers before finding sobriety and a new life as a country editor in Kentucky. Featured as a cover story in the magazine in 1974, this was a career turning point for me, leading to opportunities beyond Logan County in public broadcasting, civic life and government service. Later in 1974, when KET started *Comment on Kentucky* with an obscure rural editor—me—as host, John Ed, who was a journalistic celebrity, became a frequent panelist and attracted many viewers.

Although it is Pearce the political writer who was featured in the papers in his last decades, he should be remembered for a time when Kentuckians of all persuasions enjoyed his down-home essays in the Sunday *Courier-Journal*. He had the touch for recalling the kindness of a neighbor, the change of seasons, the bloom of romance at sweet sixteen, the death of a mother and the glow of a harvest moon on an Appalachian mountain.

John Ed had a precious talent for empathy. He could "read" people, listen to them talk about the ups and downs of their lives and then write it back for all of us to read, his prose so affecting as he graced the stories of others with the music and the mysteries of his own.

# Part V

# *The Wars They Fought*

## *Chapter 14*

# Letters Home

*I should say that the greatest fear the ordinary man has going into action is the fear that he will show he is afraid—not to his officers, or to the Germans, or to the folks back home, but to his mates with whom he has laughed and scoffed at anger. It's the elbow-to-elbow influence that carries men up to face machine guns and gas.*
—Best o' Luck, *a 1917 memoir by Alexander McClintock of Lexington, severely wounded as a volunteer overseas with the Canadian Army, decorated for Distinguished Conduct, committed suicide on June 23, 1918.*

*November 10, 2009*

Of approximately eighty-four thousand Kentuckians who served in World War I, the last veteran of the era, Robley Henry Rex, died April 28, 2009, at 107. He died at the Louisville Veterans Administration Medical Center where he attracted national attention and awards as a volunteer worker several days a week, even until age 105. (Almost two years later, Frank Buckles of West Virginia, the last living U.S. World War I veteran, died at 110 on February 27, 2011. The "last man standing" of four million Americans who went into that conflict, including my father, Albert Smith Sr., Buckles was an ambulance driver in Europe in what became known as "the Great War.")

Robley Rex was an uncle of my friend Gordon Foster of Logan County, the husband of JoAnn Taylor Foster who was our advertising manager in Russellville. For stories I began to write in the 1990s about the shrinking ranks of World War I veterans in Kentucky, I telephoned "Uncle Robley," as Gordon called him, for each of several years, marveling at his energy and continued commitment to padding down the halls at the VA hospital to cheer up younger veterans and ply them with toiletries and magazines.

The last Kentucky VA pensioner who was serving on French soil on Armistice Day 1918 was Chancey Wheeler of Maysville, who was too hard of hearing for a conversation when I called him in 1998 at a nursing home for an eightieth anniversary story of the Armistice on November 11, 1918. But on that date eighty years after the eleventh hour of the eleventh day of the eleventh month when the guns of World War I fell silent across the Western Front in France, there were only eleven Kentucky veterans of that war in the pension files of the Louisville VA office.

Two years later, the History Channel broadcast a program, "Dear Home: Letters from World War I," dramatizing the words of servicemen and woman who were on the front lines, including my father. Their eyewitness accounts often came to their families in battered, dirty envelopes marked "Somewhere in France." Expressing more intimately than a newsreel or a newspaper what it was like to fight fear, fatigue, boredom and longing for home, the letters are a poignant reminder of the horrific trench warfare almost a century ago.

My father, who enlisted from Cookeville, Tennessee, was determined to win the approval of his patriotic parents whose weekly paper strongly supported the war. But after being gassed, experiencing his horse shot out from under him and going through three weeks of combat without a bath or change of clothes, he wrote his younger brother to stay out of the army and avoid becoming cannon fodder. "You only think you want to come over here," he wrote. "This is pure unadulterated hell."

Some of the returning veterans became part of the Lost Generation described in the literature of the 1920s and '30s, but my father's contemporaries provided the leadership that saw us through the Great Depression and another world war.

In Lexington, World War I is remembered at Memorial Hall, constructed at UK in 1928, whose walls are lined with the names of 1,007 students, alumni and faculty who served. Of the 890 Kentuckians killed, 8 were from UK.

Ironically, more soldiers would die at Camp Zachery Taylor in Louisville than were Kentuckians killed overseas, and the killer was disease, writes historian James C. Klotter, an invaluable source for some of my stories of times past. After an extremely cold winter the previous year, the Spanish

Soldiers leaving at Lexington railroad station for World War I missions. *Courtesy of UK Special Collections.*

influenza struck Kentucky in late 1918; at Camp Taylor, 11,000 became ill. Sick soldiers lay on the floor, in the absence of available cots, writes Klotter in *Kentucky, Portrait in Paradox: 1900-1950.* Nurses and doctors were stricken, and some died. An estimated 1,500 soldiers died at the base. Amazingly, as the epidemic finally closed in 1919, nearly 14,000 persons had died directly due to influenza in Kentucky in 1919–18.

In Lexington Cemetery is the grave of Major General George B. Duncan, son of a Civil War mayor of Lexington. He commanded two divisions and recommended my father's friend Sergeant Alvin York for the Medal of Honor.

And at 540 East Third Street, there is the Charles Young Community center and park, named for the third African American graduate of West Point. When the army tried to kick the colonel out on a phony physical to avoid giving him command over whites, he rode a horse from Chillicothe, Ohio, to Washington, D.C., to prove his fitness.

Talk about heroes!

As I myself was aging, I suspect my increasing interest in the dwindling ranks of World War I veterans was a way of reaching out to the ghost of my

Albert Smith Sr., father of the author, served in combat overseas in World War I while his father, Rutledge Smith, a former newspaper man and railroad executive, directed the Tennessee Selective Service program as a major on active duty. *Courtesy of Smith family.*

father, who died in 1968 at seventy-one, and with whom I had a conflicted relationship. No doubt, our troubles were compounded from early on by his alcoholism, and, later, my own, but when he died, we were at peace with each other, and I had discovered, through his letters home from war, a young man, in many ways still a boy, but a very brave one—a person, says my sister Robin, "whom we hardly knew."

*Chapter 15*

# The Christian Cornet Player

*May 27, 2001*

In May 2001, still obsessed with thoughts about the struggles of my father's generations, I attended the visitation for one of the few surviving Kentucky veterans of World War I, a man I did not know named Robert H. Hall. He was 102 and one of the 12,584 Kentucky African Americans who served in that war. Of the 84,172 Kentuckians in uniform, black and white, about 6,000 went overseas, according to historian James C. Klotter. Some 890 were killed in action; 1,528 died from accidents or disease

Introducing myself to members of the family, I learned that Mr. Hall was born on August 12, 1898, in Centreville and had enlisted as an army musician. He played the cornet in a segregated band unit based in South Carolina under a white director. After the war, he became a brick mason but played music for the male chorus of his church, Lexington Main Street Baptist. A community leader, he served the church for seventy-six year as deacon and fifty years as treasurer. When his funeral was held on May 19, 2001, there were only two Kentucky men remaining on the VA list of World War I pensioners.

His son, Robert Hall Jr., said that his father's mother, Elizabeth, who was married to Lewis Hall, told him when he was a child that "she was six years old when President Lincoln freed the slaves." The elder Hall's parents were children of the Civil War era when 24,000 black Kentuckians, 60 percent of the state's black men of military age, joined the Union army. This was the second largest recruitment of blacks in any state and 13 percent of the total 178,895 blacks who fought with the Union.

Historic Main Street Baptist, where the funeral was held, is next door to the Mary Todd Lincoln home, now a museum, the Civil War home of Mrs. Abraham Lincoln's family.

## Chapter 16

# Heroes of World War II

*June 6, 2004*

In a time of growing discontent over war and politics, the week that began with the dedication of the World War II Memorial and ends on the sixtieth anniversary of the D-Day invasion recalls an era of American unity, impassioned political leadership and inspiring heroes.

This past week's oratory, while evoking little of the uplift of Roosevelt or Churchill, focused our hearts and minds on a time when we were more together as a nation, and when calls for sacrifice were heard by civilians as well as military personnel.

Along with several hundred other Kentuckians, I was at the dedication ceremonies on the Washington Mall last week. It seemed to me that the most moving moment was when the program ended—the fly-over of fighter planes on the last notes of "The Star-Spangled Banner," the spectacle of 150,000 folks turning to leave, but still cheering, the beribboned old veterans in wheel chairs rolling across the grass and the realization that, indeed, we who had been in another place six decades ago were here in this place, on this hallowed ground, still alive, by God, to remember and be remembered.

So emotional were those closing moments that one of my Kentucky companions, Howard Gray of Lexington, whipped out a cell phone and called an elderly cousin back in Glasgow, Dr. Billy Bryant, who had fought in the Philippines. Howard greeted his cousin with these words, "Billy, we are at the World War II Memorial. I just want to say, 'Thank you.'"

Of some 300,000 Kentuckians who served in World War II, about 8,000 were lost. On today's D-Day anniversary, fewer than five million of the 16 million World War II veterans survive, perhaps 75,000 from Kentucky. The youngest of us are in our late seventies, and we are dying at a rate of 1,100 a day.

Comparing public commitment in World War II to the divisiveness over Iraq, Charles P. Roland, a University of Kentucky historian, author and a former combat officer, says that "Pearl Harbor lit a torch" in the Japanese attack of December 7, 1941. "Then the same week, Hitler committed one of the stupidest blunders in history by declaring war against the U.S. There was no doubt about our enemies. And at the end, the discoveries of the Nazi death camps and the murder of millions of Jews sanctified our cause in that war."

In our group attending World War II Memorial ceremonies last week, three of us, although not in the landings, had vivid memories of D-Day. Lois Gray, of Lexington, Howard's mother, had joined the navy after college and was working at a command center in Washington. I was a seventeen-year-old volunteer in uniform for only a week. My wife, Martha Helen, was only six at D-Day, but she knew the anguish of war. Her father, Dr. Hugh B. Disharoon, an army colonel and medical doctor, had died of viral pneumonia at Fort Benning, Georgia, ten months before the invasion. He was thirty-three.

Within less than a year after D-Day, in May 1945, the German Reich was finished. Japan surrendered in August of 1945. Of the Americans serving, 400,000 had perished. Surely none of those who were killed or survived would have called themselves "the greatest generation," but their lives were of consequence, even if known only to their closest loved ones. Here are a few of their stories:

On D-Day 1944, Lois Howard was a twenty-two-year-old officer in the WAVES, the newly organized branch for women in the navy. "We all wanted to do something for our country," she said.

Lieutenant Howard was not on a ship steaming to battle, but as a mapmaker in the Office of Naval Intelligence she was escorted to and from her Washington apartment by a marine guard to chart the daily positions of the fleet. She worked with Admiral Ernest J. King, Commander-in-Chief, United States Fleet.

From bases in England sixty years ago, Colonel Phillip Ardery of Paris, Kentucky had already flown over twenty-five combat missions as a bomber pilot and qualified to go home to a wife and son. But on the eve of the

Lieutenant Lois Howard of Glasgow was an officer in the navy, serving in Washington in navy intelligence where she applied her art skills to daily plotting of ship locations in combat operations. *Courtesy of Gray family.*

*Left*: Philip Ardery, World War II flying hero from Paris, Kentucky, was a colonel at D-Day, rising after the war to major general in the Air National Guard. He became a prominent lawyer in Louisville, an advocate for liberal causes and a tireless fundraiser to fight mental illness and heart disease. He died July 26, 2012, at ninety-eight. *Courtesy of Ardery family.*

*Opposite*: Glider pilot Perry Lee Jr. of Middlesboro, Kentucky, son of a coal miner, flew one mission on D-Day, returned to England, then died in a crash on his third mission. He left a young wife and son. A brother, Joe, enlisting to avenge his death, went to college on the GI Bill, then law school and became a nationally respected bankruptcy judge and is in the UK Law School Hall of Fame. *Courtesy of Lee family.*

invasion, he volunteered for one more mission. Flying in the dark in a highly dangerous close formation, the 200 planes he led scattered fragmentation bombs to help clear the beaches of mines and explosives planted by command of Field Marshal Erwin Rommel.

Ardery made it home. "I used up somebody else's luck," he said. But Perry Lee Jr. of Middlesboro, another kind of airman, a glider pilot, ran out of luck. Lee, the son of a Middlesboro coal miner, had learned to fly gliders at Bowman Field in Louisville. In the Normandy invasion, he safely flew one sortie over the beaches to land infantrymen behind the lines. Making his way back to England, he then flew a second mission. Three months later, he was killed when his craft crashed in Holland. Of the glider pilots, 25 percent died in combat flights. Perry Lee was only twenty-one, but his survivors included a young wife and an infant son.

On D-Day, Captain Joseph A. Hicks, an army combat engineer, was ordered to go in on the very first landing ahead of the infantry and blast away wire, land mines and concrete obstacles. A veteran of eight campaigns and three earlier invasions, in one of which he received a battlefield promotion, Hicks doubted if he would live to see his wife and daughter back in Hopkinsville. Miraculously, he did survive and later told his story to Cornelius Ryan, author of the book and movie on D-Day *The Longest Day.* "I figured I was a fugitive from the law of averages," Hicks said.

A choppy weather crisis in the English Channel faced General Dwight Eisenhower before he gave the "Go" for Overlord, the most ambitious amphibious assault in history in the bloodiest war in history. Seven thousand ships, 11,000 aircraft and 150,000 troops converged on the Normandy coast.

Allied casualties in twenty-four-hour assault at D-Day are put at between 10,000 and 12,000. The figure 6,603 is given by author Ryan for American casualties, with 1,500 killed, 3,200 wounded and 2,000 missing. Estimates of the German losses ranged from 4,000 to 9,000. At the end of June, Rommel reported his losses for the month were "28 generals, 354 commanders, and approximately 250,000 men."

Of course, the invasion was the long awaited turning point of the war, the consequences of which involved social and political as well dramatic technological and scientific change. Seeds for social change were certainly planted for African Americans, who fought in uniform while treated as second-class citizens, and for women, who made up about 2 percent of the armed forces.

In Russellville, where I edited a small weekly paper, Moses Gaines, an African American navy veteran who worked in the local Coca-Cola bottling plant, shared an enduring friendship formed in wartime with Otis Singletary, who died last year in retirement after serving for eighteen years as president of the University of Kentucky. As Gaines and Singletary separately explained to me, Singletary, a lieutenant from Mississippi, championed the cause of Gaines and other black men who, as mess stewards, were denied gunnery training on their quartermaster ship. "We were sailors and not allowed to fight," Gaines told me. "But Dr. Singletary fought for us. He turned that ship order around, and we got training and battle stations."

In civilian life, Lois Howard became the wife of James N. Gray, also a veteran, who died at age fifty-four in 1972, leaving Lois a widow with six children and a struggling construction company. Now one of the leading design-build companies in the United States, Gray Construction grew, her children believe, because their mother had learned in the navy, as her son Jim Gray, the CEO, says, "women do not have to accept limits on their abilities or opportunities."

Navy veteran Moses Gaines of Russellville, Kentucky, with his World War II friend and champion Otis Singletary, who brought him war mementoes on a visit to Russellville. Singletary became president of UK. Gaines went to work for Coca-Cola. Photo by Terry Birdwhistell, *Courtesy of the* Courier-Journal.

A grateful Congress created in the GI Bill, the greatest government investment ever for the future of this country, through education and subsidized housing for veterans. Back home, attorney Phillip Ardery, now of Louisville, represented rural electric cooperatives that turned on the lights in thousands of Kentucky farms. Joe Hicks built a fertilizer company in Russellville that prospered with the farmers. Perry Lee's brother Joe, also a veteran, became a distinguished federal judge after going to college on the GI Bill, which also supported the educations of academics Charlie Roland and Otis Singletary.

Educated as military orphans by the GI Bill's provisions, my wife and her sister Ginny Lawson, of Hopkinsville, have been civic leaders in their hometowns. Martha Helen's multiple talents have generously compensated for my deficiencies as a part-time businessman while I practiced journalism as a kind of full-time public scold—forever looking for the kind of visionary leadership that we experienced in my youth, that which inspired us to victory at D-Day and richly rewarded us in peace.

# Part VI

# *A Special Time*

## Chapter 17

# FDR in Kentucky

*April 30, 2005*

This month, as a Louisville church hosted a national telecast rallying Americans against Democrats opposed to President Bush's ultra-conservative court nominees, older Kentuckians remember another April, sixty years ago, when churches all over this state and nation—indeed, over most of the world were praying in remembrance of a Democratic leader who had just died.

On April 12, 1945, the news flashed from Warm Springs, Georgia, that Franklin Delano Roosevelt had died of a cerebral hemorrhage at his vacation home. Only six weeks past his sixty-third birthday and exhausted from a dozen years as the thirty-second president, he died on the crest of victory in World War II and at the end of the Great Depression, whose challenges had propelled him into office when fifteen million Americans were unemployed.

In Louisville, on the hour of his funeral, streetcars and buses halted; phone service shut down. It is almost impossible to imagine the sorrow in this country on that weekend.

A year later, when I was transferred to Fort Knox to help open a Field Artillery training center, I was around when older GIs came home as veterans to renew their lives in Kentucky. In today's political language, Kentucky was a solid "blue state" of Democratic voters loyal to the memory of Roosevelt—his New Deal programs that they believed had rescued them from farm and home foreclosures, job losses and downright hunger in the

President Franklin D. Roosevelt, at his desk in wartime, had many influential supporters in Kentucky, among them Senator Alben Barkley and Russellville politico Thomas S. Rhea. Beginning a cross-country trip in 1938, FDR stopped the train to make a brief speech in Russellville, vividly recalled by old-timers when Al Smith became the editor there twenty years later. *Courtesy of the Library of Congress.*

Depression and his leadership that triumphed in the war and made us the strongest country on earth.

But this past week, on the Sunday when religious conservatives aired their complaints against the Democratic Party from a Louisville pulpit, Kentucky's venerable historian laureate, Thomas D. Clark, turned his thoughts, in an interview at his Lexington home, to the impact of FDR's New Deal on this state. He noted, also, "the irony of it" that a leading figure in the religious right's "Justice Sunday" attacks, Dr. Bill Frist, is majority leader of the U.S. Senate. In Roosevelt's era, this was the same powerful office held by Kentucky's Alben Barkley, who guided FDR's social security legislation into law—the pillar of the New Deal that President Bush and Frist propose to change with partial privatization.

Barkley, who became President Harry Truman's vice president, was one of a half dozen or so Kentuckians Dr. Clark remembered as prominent Roosevelt supporters. Among them were Congressman Fred Vinson and Solicitor General Stanley Reed, both of whom would move to the U.S. Supreme Court. From the west and east sides of Kentucky, were three other congressmen, the Gregory brothers of Mayfield—first William V. and then Noble Gregory—and Andrew Jackson May of Prestonsburg. Together, they battled for the New Deal, with one notable exception: They split over the Tennessee Valley Authority. The Gregorys wanted TVA dams and lakes and cheap public power; May was vehemently opposed, fearing hydroelectric power would undercut the coal industry and destroy Kentucky Utilities and its coal-generated electric services. (TVA backers prevailed of course, but May was wrong: TVA also built coal plants and became the largest consumer of Kentucky coal.)

The New Deal farm, forest and conservation programs were favored by the *Courier-Journal* publisher Robert Worth Bingham, whose loyalty FDR rewarded by naming him ambassador to England. In the president's inner circle, Marvin McIntyre of La Grange and the gifted young Edward F. Prichard Jr. of Paris were aides with access to FDR.

While acknowledging the influence of United States senator Mitch McConnell in today's Washington and over Republican politics at home, Clark says that Kentucky "played a stronger role" in shaping the country's destiny under Roosevelt than it does under George W. Bush.

Clark, retired from the University of Kentucky and author of over two dozen books, will be 102 in July when the new Kentucky History Center in Frankfort will be renamed for him. He sees three great achievements of the New Deal in Kentucky:

- The "awakening of a spark of interest in education," building schools ("Every college got some kind of building"), supporting students with jobs to keep them in classes and thus employing teachers.
- Transforming the land with conservation practices and rural electrification that "lifted the burden of living and enhanced domestic life," giving farmers back their independence with various programs…some helpful, some "wrongheaded" but always insisting they would not be abandoned to market pressures manipulated by business interests.
- New regulations to rehabilitate banks and stabilize financial institutions (one hundred of which had failed in the commonwealth).

Did the New Deal—branded as socialism by FDR's enemies—save the country, or did World War II save the New Deal and end the Depression? "You could put a dozen people in a room, and they would take exception to me," says Clark, "but there were major achievements and effective leadership, and Kentucky politicians were in the thick of it."

Historian George T. Blakey, author of the book *Hard Times and New Deal in Kentucky, 1929–39* and various articles on the Depression, counts these achievements: food and relief money for 500,000 desperate Kentuckians; jobs for thousands more who built 14,000 miles of improved highways, 9,000 public buildings and 600 projects that included the Student Union at University of Kentucky, the prison at LaGrange and the gold depository at Fort Knox; the enrollment of 80,000 young men in the Civilian Conservation Corps (CCC) who, working from fifty-nine camps in the state, developed Mammoth Cave, the Dupont Lodge at Cumberland Falls, the amphitheater at Pine Mountain and much more; saving homes and farms with new financing agencies that benefited over 60,000 Kentuckians for whom all other options had vanished; subsidies for 250,000 farmers; low-cost housing projects in cities and a 400 percent increase in electrification of farms; the massive Kentucky Dam enterprise by TVA, which affected the entire state; reforms of working conditions, and support for union rights.

In Hopkinsville, my wife and her sister, whose father, an army doctor, had died, grew up in the shadow of Fort Campbell, which the Roosevelt administration had cunningly sited on the Kentucky-Tennessee border to benefit the economy for political supporters in both states.

In Russellville, when I was editor of the weekly *News-Democrat*, my friend and the local bottler Joe Copple told me that he obtained the Coca-Cola franchise at Fort Campbell after the legendary Logan County political boss Thomas S. Rhea introduced him to the commanding general and boasted of a White House conference at which he had bragged on the troops to President Roosevelt.

After Roosevelt's last appearance in Louisville, when he spoke to fifteen thousand people on July 8, 1938, Rhea and Barkley joined him on the train as it headed west for a cross continent trip to the Pacific coast. "I have a surprise for you," the president told his friends. "Send the word ahead, and I'll stop at Russellville and give a little talk."

At 10:00 p.m., when the train pulled into the Russellville station, an estimated six thousand to eight thousand people were waiting, according to Edward Coffman Jr., a retired minister and local historian, who was in the high school band that greeted the president.

Coffman, who grew up in a pre-McConnell era when western Kentucky was known politically as "the Gibraltar of Democracy," admires Frist, a physician who performed a quadruple bypass on him in Nashville before he went to the Senate. "I was in a fog when I awoke," says Coffman, "and I asked him when he was going to operate, 'Oh, I did that two days ago,' Frist laughed."

Roosevelt's New Deal is estimated to have spent $1 billion in a single decade to revive the Kentucky economy. In Tennessee—which similarly benefited from FDR's programs—the Hospital Corporation of American, controlled by the Frist family, has agreed to pay the federal government $1.7 billion to settle charges of defrauding government health care programs. HCA is the largest for-profit hospital chain in America, and this is the largest government fraud settlement in history.

Frist, who admitted he had never voted until a few years before he ran for the Senate, plans to leave the Senate when his present term is up. It is widely believed he is planning to seek the presidency himself as a successor to President Bush, and that appealing to Mr. Bush's base with the religious right was one of the reasons Frist joined the Louisville church attack on Democratic senators.

But there is another view of Frist and Bush by an old New Dealer, attorney Morton Holbrook of Owensboro, who was prominent in state Democratic politics. "Roosevelt shaped our lives, saved this country," says Holbrook. "Frist and Bush are tearing down everything FDR stood for, and it is an outrage against history."

Keeping a promise to serve only two terms, Senator Frist retired in 2007. Contrary to speculation, he announced he would not seek the presidency and would return to medicine.

Unlike the Republicans in the Senate, where he was majority leader for four years, he supported aspects of President Obama's Affordable Care Act, especially the creation of state health insurance exchanges.

Over time, civil suits cost HCA more than $2 billion to settle. After departing as CEO and chairman under pressure in 1997, Rick Scott, who said he was never targeted in the probes of Columbia/HCA finances, moved to Naples, Florida. He began investing in health care, technology and manufacturing. In 2010, spending an estimated $75 to $78 million, he was elected governor of Florida, winning over a Democrat by 68,000 votes.

Dr. Clark died on June 28, 2005, at age 101, two months after the interview about the New Deal and Kentucky.

## *Chapter 18*

# Barkley and Truman

*July 12, 1998*

Today is the fiftieth anniversary of the keynote speech by United States senator Alben W. Barkley of Kentucky at the Democratic Party's convention in Philadelphia. Barkley's stem-winding attack on the Republican Party and rousing defense of sixteen years of Democratic control of the White House touched off a thirty-minute blowout on the convention floor. The one-hour speech also set the stage for President Harry S. Truman's historic upset defeat of Governor Thomas E. Dewey of New York.

In 1948, I began covering politics for the New Orleans *Times-Picayune*. It was the first election in which I voted (for Truman) and the first time I ever bet on an election (against Truman). It was also my maiden effort at following a U.S. Senate race. As assistant state editor, I reported on the campaign of Russell B. Long, the twenty-nine-year-old son of the late Huey "Kingfish" Long, whose narrow victory over a rural judge named Robert "Fighting Bob" Kennon was stolen, some said, by Russell Long's uncle, the wildly eccentric Governor Earl K. Long. (If this is confusing, remember the movie *Blaze*. Paul Newman was Uncle Earl.)

When the Dixiecrats in Louisiana forced Truman's name from the Democratic ballot, and Earl Long, a party loyalist, had to call a special session of the legislature to get the president back on, I was there. I was also in New Orleans when Barkley courageously flew in to stump for Truman and not a single prominent politician showed up. Only a handful of labor leaders and a few Jewish folks who appreciated his support of Israel greeted Barkley in a state he knew his ticket would lose.

The issue there, and all over the South, was race, equal opportunity. So successful were the segregationists that until I came to Kentucky ten years later to edit the Russellville paper, I had never seen blacks and whites playing basketball together.

But earlier in 1948, there was that stirring Barkley keynote speech scorching the "other party," which he said would bring back the days "when the spiders were so weak from starvation that they could not weave a cobweb." When he finished, without benefit of air-conditioning and under the sweltering lights of the first televised national political convention, Kentucky delegates poured out of their seats and into the aisles.

Led by Governor Earle C. Clements and carrying placards proclaiming "Barkley for Vice President," the Kentuckians marched at the head of a procession that swelled as they circled the hall five times. By the time Barkley, the acting convention chairman, had finally gaveled the crowd back to order, he had been joined on the platform by many of the party's congressional leaders. They included House Speaker Sam Rayburn and Senator Tom Connally of Texas, Senators Lister Hill and John Sparkman of Alabama and Representative James "Jimmy" Roosevelt of California—under whose father, the late President Franklin D. Roosevelt, Barkley had served as a Senate majority leader.

Barkley, a sharecropper's son born in a log cabin in Western Kentucky, was already esteemed as one of the nation's greatest political orators. Having twice before been a convention keynoter, he had to be begged for this speech—especially in a year when Truman had grown immensely unpopular and every political pundit was predicting a landslide for Dewey, the Republican nominee whose party had laid groundwork by recapturing both chambers of Congress in 1946.

On the Sunday before Barkley's address, Philadelphia taxi drivers joked that the Democrats were so dispirited "they need a hearse, not a cab." Clearly, many delegates—maybe a majority—wished for another presidential candidate. There was still a "Draft Ike" boom, although United States Army general Dwight D. Eisenhower had already disclaimed any intention of accepting nomination.

Truman was so disliked that liberals in the North and conservatives in the South were threatening to form separate tickets. As a border-state senator who had supported FDR's New Deal in the Depression and Truman's 1948 initiatives for civil rights, Barkley was probably the only figure who could

President Harry Truman (right) on the 1948 campaign train with Kentucky's U.S. senator Alben Barkley, when most of the press and pollsters gave them no hope of winning. In Kentucky, as elsewhere, the "experts" seemed heedless of the enormous crowds that turned out for the Democrats—an estimated ninety thousand folks saw Truman on stops from Henderson to Ashland, with nine thousand in Lexington alone. Barkley crisscrossed the country by plane. He flew 150,000 miles and delivered 250 speeches, mostly in small cities—farm, coal and railroad towns. Back in his hometown of Paducah to vote, he confided to a friend, Henry Ward, his belief that "we are not going to make it." But he was wrong. They did. *Photo from National Park Service, Abbie Rowe, Courtesy of Harry S. Truman Library.*

lift the clouds from that convention, ignite the party's hopes and bring the delegates to their feet cheering.

Back at the White House, a curiously conflicted president watched the proceedings on a twelve-inch screen on the newly installed Dumont TV and mused that the address, which so moved the convention, "sounded like a man who would like to be president himself." Only once had Barkley mentioned Truman by name.

After all, there had been rivalries between the two men, and Truman was well aware that but for a temporary falling out between Barkley and FDR before the 1944 Democratic convention Barkley might have been FDR's choice for vice president. Then Barkley, not Truman, would have become president when FDR died April 12, 1945.

Still, it was Barkley just hours after FDR's death who told Truman to stop deprecating his ability to carry on. It was Barkley, Truman's leader when both were senators, who said, "Quit calling me 'boss.' Have confidence in yourself. If you do not, the people will lose confidence in you."

Truman picked up the phone and called Philadelphia, but Barkley had gone to bed. Until then, Truman had wanted a stronger liberal, Justice William Douglas, who was younger than he, but Douglas declined, reportedly telling friends he didn't want to be a No. 2 to a No. 2 man.

At seventy-one, Barkley was seven years older than Truman. As a Kentuckian, he offered no geographical balance to Truman's home state of Missouri, but this was brushed aside when Truman finally reached him. If he was finally to be nominated, said Barkley, who had coveted the honor since 1928, it had better come quickly. "I don't want it passed around until it is like a cold biscuit."

The next day, July 14, a floor fight turned angry as a militant faction of liberals headed by Minneapolis mayor Hubert Humphrey pressed for and won the first unequivocal civil rights plank in a Democratic platform.

Speaking less than ten minutes, Humphrey made history. It was time to move forward. "There are those who say to you we are rushing this issue of civil rights," Humphrey said. "I say we are 172 years late. The time has arrived for the Democratic Party to get out of the shadow of states' rights and walk forthrightly into the bright sunshine of human rights."

Of course, this sparked a Southern states bolt, but not all of Dixie was resistant. Barkley said the South was more open-minded than the Dixiecrats admitted.

Half a century later, recollecting Barkley's role for that occasion may help us measure the appeals and potential of this year's candidates for a U.S. Senate seat from Kentucky. Why was he such a force? It was certainly more than partisanship or rhetoric or stamina or wit, although they abounded.

Perhaps it was optimism. In dark times, he promised brighter days, and the words were persuasive—as simple as that.

*Chapter 19*

# Patriots

When I was a boy in Sarasota, Florida, in the 1930s, we always turned out for the Fourth of July American Legion picnics—hats, hands on hearts for the flag. At home that night, after the barbecue, beer and speeches, Dad would pull down the World War I army book and boozily name his buddies in the pictures from France until he fell asleep.

When my father finally gave up on Florida, with its vacant, weedy, saltwater lots, its sandspurs and broken dreams, we returned to Tennessee for a new beginning on a hardscrabble farm that my grandfather Rutledge Smith bought after Dad promised to quit drinking. This was in the middle of the Great Depression. I was twelve. People were losing jobs, going hungry and war was breaking out in Europe again, but there was hope and faith—because President Roosevelt and my Grandmother Graeme said so.

Of course, we all thought FDR was inspiring (ignoring two sorehead uncles), but in Nashville, Graeme was the best orator around. A former schoolteacher and editor of my grandfather's mountain paper before they went on to bigger things in the city, Graeme was an indefatigable leader of the patriotic Daughters of the American Revolution, Daughters of the War of 1812 and the United Daughters of the Confederacy. She provided inspiration to spark the uplift on public occasions, especially July 4, when she was a human firecracker.

So fervently did my grandmother tend the memorial flames for past wars, my grandfather said she had become the family's "old battle ax." The thought of peace, he jested "disturbs her mind."

Despite his scoffing, Grandfather, known as "the Major" for his World War I service, was right there with my father and the other veterans in Legion caps when Graeme stood up in the cemeteries on July 4 to recall for anyone who would listen the bravery of Andrew Jackson, Sam Houston and Tennessee's special favorite Sergeant Alvin York, the former conscientious objector who killed or captured all those Germans and who was portrayed by Gary Cooper in the movie.

After Pearl Harbor, Graeme commanded me to pick up her flag. When I was fifteen, she coached me to victory in the national American Legion High School Oratorical Contest and to a college scholarship (that I never got around to using because, like my father before me, she also drove me to drink, but that's another story and perhaps unfair. Family genes were also at play, and two other of her children and a foster son were highly successful without the drama to which my father and I were given). When I was finally old enough to go down to the Union station to catch the train to the army, Graeme handed me a Bible in which she had penned her eternal devotion because (in capital letters) I was volunteering TO FIGHT. She really was a scrapper.

My grandmother died in a car accident in 1949, disappointed with me because I decided to become a reporter instead of governor, but the Major soldiered on. At Christmas 1961, when he was ninety-two, he was still recalling his Confederate father, Captain Walton Smith, shot through both legs at the Battle of Chickamauga, and his grandfather Thomas Jefferson Smith, who followed Jackson to the Battle of New Orleans. A bit of a boaster, the old Major reminded me of his friendship with the Wright brothers, then mentioned space flights—"I'm up on Sputnik," he said. We sat by the fireplace at his Nashville home where he hung a rifle from every American war—except the one we would lose, along with our innocence about patriotism, the war in Vietnam, the consequences of which he would not be "up on."

Next summer, the Major was gone, and then my father died. Although he had not quit drinking, Dad had finally outwitted that rocky old farm—by selling it for a subdivision near the new Old Hickory Lake. My widowed mother observed that most of her neighbors in the new homes owned two cars and a boat and supported Richard Nixon. On our last drive around that lake, she grumbled that none of them recognized who provided the amenities for their good life.

"Who was that¸ Mama?" I asked, teasing. "President Roosevelt gave us all this," she said, wearily waving toward Johnny Cash's brightly lit house at Hendersonville. "With the TVA."

"Edison invented the light bulb," I said. "Don't get smart with me, Albert," she replied. "You know what I mean."

Next day, she died in her sleep, the last member of our family who passionately believed that government had made life better.

# Part VII
## *In Black and White*

# *Chapter 20*

# Blues and Jazz

When I was a child of six or seven in Sarasota, my young mother, Elvira Mace Smith, whose nickname was "Muff," took to her bed with clinical depression in the Great Depression for a month but was cheered with an invitation from her bachelor brother, Robin Mace, a Goldman Sachs stock broker, to visit him in Detroit.

When she returned several weeks later, after a check-up at Detroit's Ford Hospital, she had rallied, somewhat. A prescription—in those pre-Prozac days, for a mid-afternoon glass of sherry with a dollop of raw eggs—seemed to help, but she thrilled me with stories of theater-going in Detroit, especially to see Ethel Waters on stage. Perhaps it was the road show of Irving Berlin's *As Thousands Cheer*—I don't recall—but hearing Waters, one of the great blues singers, was a favorite story my mother repeatedly told.

I remembered this when I walked into the Old Absinthe House on Bourbon Street in New Orleans where Waters had a nightly gig in November 1947, the month I took the Greyhound to Nashville after dropping out of Vanderbilt.

I was twenty years old, with $100 in my pocket to get by on until I found some kind of job (in writing, I hoped). Without telling my parents I was quitting Vandy, I had also left behind the GI Bill benefits and a national scholarship, won in a high school speech contest, to find a life more accommodating than college to my developing alcoholism.

A week later, after spending half of my $100 to hear Waters sing some of her signature songs—"Stormy Weather," "Cabin in the Sky," "Taking

A pioneering African American entertainer in segregated America, Ethel Waters was successful on the stage, screen, TV and in nightclubs. Her musical styling greatly influenced twentieth-century blues and jazz, expressive as it was of a turbulent complex personal life and career, which ended with her singing gospels on the Billy Graham crusades. *Courtesy of Gottlieb Collection, Library of Congress.*

a Chance on Love"—I was sleeping in a shabby rented room on the edge of the French Quarter. I had a copy boy's job paying $22.50 a week at the *Times-Picayune.*

I nearly starved on that meager salary, but I was sipping the occasional complimentary drink from Owen Brennan, the owner of the Absinthe House and my first new friend in New Orleans. Next year, as Brennan opened what would become a storied restaurant, I was promoted to a copy editor at the

*Times-Picayune* and wrote a freelance article for *Newsweek*'s music section on jazz reborn in the city that gave it to the world. Perhaps impressed by the crowds lined up for Waters at the Absinthe House, Bourbon Street was now convinced that people would pay for "that music," and clubs were hiring bands both black and white.

A white band, Sharkey Bonano and his Kings of Dixieland, held forth at Hyp Guinle's Famous Door, and our editor took Tallulah Bankhead to hear Oscar (Papa) Celestin's all-black Tuxedo Jazz Band at Steve Valenti's Paddock Lounge. The father of Al Hirt, a popular trumpet player, was a retired cop who cashed my "cold" checks at the police credit union where he was treasurer and held them until I could cover them after payday.

While "the good times rolled," eating and drinking was segregated, and African Americans not only went to the back of the bus or streetcar but the taxicabs were also separate for black and white. The longshoremen's union on the docks was split by race just like the schools. To attract Ethel Waters to perform at the Absinthe House, Brennan confided to me, he created a private apartment upstairs. The newspapers so ignored aspirations for civil rights and other concerns of African Americans that when *Fortune* magazine printed an article about seven black millionaires in New Orleans after I came to Kentucky, I had never heard of them.

Daughter from the rape of a thirteen-year-old girl in Pennsylvania, Ethel Waters had the meanest of childhoods. In fact, "I never was a child," she said. "I was never cuddled, or liked, or understood by my family." Despite all this, she began singing professionally at seventeen and had a rapid rise in show business, eventually starring on stage, in movies and TV and nightclubs. A biography, *His Eye is on the Sparrow*, was a bestseller. She is acclaimed with Louie Armstrong and Sophie Tucker as one of the trinity from which modern and popular jazz singing sprang in the early twentieth century.

I cannot say I lifted a finger in my troubled, self-indulgent twenties to champion civil rights in New Orleans. The best I did was nothing—except to be polite and admire black talent. In Kentucky, recovered from booze, I was fortunate to have journalistic encounters with maybe twenty African American leaders and artists as well as white activists who made a brave difference during those years while I was making a fool of myself.

At Berea College I met Julian Bond, Alex Haley and Maya Angelou. At UK I filmed an interview with Alexander Young of Atlanta and shared a forum at Transylvania University with the Reverend Fred Shutttlesworth who was nearly murdered in Birmingham. In Nashville, Aaron Henry, the black dentist from Clarksdale, Mississippi, recalled co-founding the Mississippi Freedom Party with journalist Hodding Carter III, who had worked for me as a college intern in New Orleans. "The color down there is now all green, like money," he told me.

I never saw Ethel Waters again, except on TV, an ailing elderly black lady in a white dress on a platform with the Reverend Billy Graham as a part of his evangelistic crusades. So much of the "Stormy Weather" she sang about in her youth now a memory, she was praising the God of her gospel music, a vision of heaven where maybe my mother, also a woman of faith, would hear her thrilling voice once more.

## *Chapter 21*

# Rights, Ray and Russellville

For many years, a cedar tree on the Adairville road south of Russellville was known as "the hanging tree," because of two separate lynchings there, one in 1897 of three white men accused of murder, then in 1908 when four black men were taken by a mob from the county jail in their night clothes and hung from the same tree.

Early in my tenure as editor of the paper, an old white lady renewing her subscription casually told me she was a daughter of the farmer whose fatal shooting by a black tenant set off the 1908 lynchings. My customer revealed no rancor in her story. It was so long ago, and I guess she figured I had heard it already—most people had. A gruesome photograph of the dead black men was printed on postcards and circulated through the mails for years until the postal service said "No more!" But worse than that, the lynch victims had nothing to do with her father's death. They were arrested on suspicion after false rumors circulated of a black "uprising" over the arrest of the tenant who shot her father. That man, who was hidden from the mob by the jailer's son and a deputy, eventually received a life sentence and died in prison.

Race relations improved in the county after the Rhea family's courthouse Democratic machine defeated a slate of candidates endorsed by the Ku Klux Klan in 1925. When I came to Russellville, the city and county high schools had integrated, voluntarily, and the elementary schools soon followed. This was only four years after the Supreme Court's historic *Brown v. Board* decision, but I was told that, unlike what happened when I was in the Deep South, the local lawyers advised the politicians they must obey the court and not make trouble—"the law is the law."

I tell this to preface two stories about race and history in modern Logan County that developed after I left to work in Washington for President Jimmy Carter, the peanut farmer who hung a portrait of Martin Luther King in the statehouse when he was governor of Georgia.

As related to me by Jim Turner, a former editor of my papers, they involve Charles Neblett, who moved to Russellville after gaining national attention with the Freedom Singers in the Civil Rights era. This was a quartet who sang songs that Neblett says "came out of jails, picket lines, churches, marches and pulling bodies out of rivers."

They sang at the 1963 March on Washington and Dr. King's "I have a dream" speech. Neblett, who turned seventy-one in 2012, moved to Logan County after marrying Marvina Benton of Russellville. He was the first African American elected as a magistrate on the Fiscal Court, the county governing body.

In February 2010, Neblett conducted workshops with First Lady Michelle Obama for two hundred children at the White House and met the president. The same year, he was inducted into the Kentucky Civil Rights Hall of Fame, the honors for which included twenty-seven arrests when he was a college student fighting to end segregation.

Meanwhile, Turner notes that next door to the house where she was raised in Russellville, the memory of Mary Ann Fisher is kept fresh each summer by the Mary Ann Fisher Concert Series in the yard of the West Kentucky African American Heritage Museum. Mary Ann and a sister were raised by Gertrude "City" Merritt, a woman of color known for her excellent cooking. Her son John Merritt was described in an obituary in our paper in 1948 as "a leader in all things for the betterment of his community." He was, of course, an ally of Democratic kingpin Thomas S. Rhea—that, too, "in all things."

Mary Ann Fisher was a blues singer who performed and recorded with Ray Charles and Marvin Gaye and also on her own. The 2004 movie *Ray*, which earned actor Jamie Foxx an Academy Award for portraying Ray Charles, included a dramatization of Fisher as one of his backup singers, the Rayettes. Fisher was reported to be unhappy with her portrayal. She died that same year and is in the Kentucky Music Hall of Fame.

"I knew her when she was with Ray Charles," Charles Neblett told Jim Turner. "We (the Freedom Singers) worked with Ray Charles several times."

The Fisher Concert Series is sponsored by Russellville Blues, organized by attorney Joe Gran Clark, a Harvard law school graduate; Michael Morrow, a local historian of African American life; Michael Gough, a singer and longtime friend of Clark; and a younger generation of community activists. I applaud them for saving stories and artifacts of the black heritage in Logan County—an overdue and valuable supplement to the focus of an older generation in the all-white Logan County Historical Society. I was president of the society in another era when we read papers to each other about dead white men who were governors of Kentucky or preached in the Great Revival of 1800.

## *Chapter 22*

# Reunion in Louisiana

*August 2, 1998*

Another chapter in the recovery of African American history was celebrated last month in Washington, D.C., with the unveiling of a memorial to the 209,000 black soldiers who fought with the Union in the Civil War. The heroic centerpiece of the bronze and graphite monument was created by Kentuckian Ed Hamilton, the modest African American sculptor hailed as "an artistic genius" by his hometown newspaper, the *Courier-Journal*.

On the Saturday that the Louisville newspaper published a picture of Hamilton being greeted in Washington by the venerable historian John Hope Franklin, my son-in-law and I were welcomed to a Louisiana plantation by Sue Lyles Eakin, a friend of Franklin and author of eight books about Louisiana, including a history which noted that during the Civil War, twenty-four thousand black troops from Louisiana served in the Union army, more than any other state.

Franklin is the Duke University historian emeritus who heads President Clinton's commission on race and reconciliation. He is black and a mentor for George Wright, formerly of Lexington and now a vice-president of the University of Texas who is Kentucky's leading African American historian. Sue Eakin, who is white and seventy-eight, has not enjoyed Franklin's prominence; but she is probably the foremost authority on the black experience on Louisiana's plantations before and after the Civil War. She is also the mother of my friend Paul Eakin, a University of Kentucky math professor who accompanied me on the trip to meet his mother and introduce her to Bill Major, my son-in-law.

The continuing struggle for equal rights in Louisiana has been a lifelong concern of Sue Eakin, as it was for me in a passive way in my ten years as a young reporter in New Orleans. Each of us, I learned on this trip, knew and was intrigued by the controversial and corrupt governor, Earl K. Long, who rose above his craziness and racist past to be remembered as an effective and courageous champion of justice for people of color. When Long became governor in 1948, 22,000 blacks were registered to vote. When I left in 1957 and he was again governor, there were 150,000 black voters — the largest number of African Americans registered in any state in the South. Long rammed through social programs that aided blacks and whites. "A poor man is a poor man," he said. Later, as his foes demagogued against voting rights and integrated schools, he jeered them in a legendary confrontation: "Don't forget the feds, they've got the atom bomb."

Bill Major is a newly appointed assistant professor of English at Louisiana State University–Eunice, a bayou country branch of LSU. He and my daughter Ginny are a commuter marriage between Maryland and Louisiana this year, while Ginny completes her last year of graduate studies. Of special interest to Bill, who will teach a course in African American literature this fall, was Sue Eakin's research for a book she edited on Solomon Northup, a New Yorker who was abducted in 1841, sold into slavery, rescued twelve years later and published an account of the story that became a best seller.

Northup's years of toil and bondage were endured not far from Walnut Grove, a lavishly restored antebellum home at Chaneyville in central Louisiana owned by Sue Eakin's sister, Wanda Elizabeth "Betty" McGowen. There, we met the sisters for an overnight visit, noticing immediately a photograph of an earlier visitor, actor Paul Newman, who was there while he was playing the role of Earl Long in the movie *Blaze*. "I told Paul Newman that Sue and I are different," Betty said over shrimp, crawfish and beer on her veranda. "She grew up wanting to help the downtrodden. I grew up wanting Walnut Grove."

Next morning, at her book-filled home in nearby Bunkie, where Paul's late father had owned the weekly newspaper, Sue Eakin showed us her life's work—hundreds of priceless photos and dozens of notebooks that chronicle a vanished society, the black families who had lived in cabins and worked the rich cotton and cane fields along the eighty miles of a meandering stream known as Bayou Boeuf (French for "ox"). This was the

Son-in-law Bill Major and Al Smith enjoy a shrimp and crawfish feast on a Louisiana plantation with host Betty McGowen and her sister Professor Sue Eakin, an authority on African American history. Bill, a UK graduate, was starting a teaching career at a branch of Louisiana State University when visited by Smith and Eakin's son Paul, a professor at UK. *Courtesy of Paul Eakin.*

culture of mule and plow that kept blacks on the land long after the Civil War, free but not free, until the tractor, the cotton baler and the cane cutter came—and drove them away.

As Sue Eakin explained, "I don't know why, but ever since I was a child living on a place called Compromise Plantation—named for a race bet—I wanted to know more about the descendants of slaves in Louisiana. Those 300,000 slaves and their work on the plantations," she said, "earned Louisiana the second-richest per capita income of any state at the outbreak of the Civil War."

At war's end, a collapsing economy and brutally restrictive state laws enacted as Union troops went home kept the whites in power and the blacks in a new kind of bondage, the era of segregation, sharecropping and store debt. The astonishing collection of materials from that era—the high-quality pictures, taped and typed interviews—was started when she was in high school sixty-five years ago and continued as she married, reared five children, wrote books and newspaper articles, obtained a doctor's degree in history at age sixty and, finally retiring, was named one of LSU's five most distinguished professors.

Driving back to the airport, I recalled 1948, when my paper wouldn't print a black person's picture unless it was Joe Louis. The owners of the *Times-Picayune* hated Earl Long, Sue Eakin said last week, "because Earl and his brother Huey [the governor and senator who was assassinated in 1935] broke the grip of the planters' political leadership, which the big papers and the politicians in the New Orleans ring supported."

Crazy Earl Long and the blacks and poor whites he helped may never get a monument, but their story about oppression and survival is preserved in that little house in Bunkie in Avoyelles parish. I'm glad Ginny and Bill, starting careers in Cajun country fifty years after I did, will have a chance to study those precious records—deep roots in the Delta's muddy truths, history that shows who was on the right side, including a few whites like Earl and Sue.

When Sue Eakin died eleven years later at ninety on September 17, 2009, at her home in Bunkie, Louisiana, she left her fabulous collection of photographs of African American life in rural Louisiana to a branch of LSU at nearby Alexandria, where she taught for many years. Her friend, John Hope Franklin, preceded her in death in March 2009. George Wright is now president of Prairie A&M College, a historically black school in Texas, the largest in his state's A&M system. Sue's sister Betty eventually sold Walnut Grove.

My daughter and her husband now live in West Hartford, Connecticut, where they are raising two daughters. A professor of English at University of Hartford, Bill has written a book, *Grounded Vision*, on agrarian ideas in the teaching of literature. Ginny completed her PhD in industrial organizational psychology and is an executive coach.

For UK, Paul Eakin was "principal investigator" for a group of professors who won a National Science Foundation grant of $25 million to improve teaching of science, technology, engineering and math (STEM) in Appalachia, and the largest such award won in Kentucky at that time. He and his wife, Scottye, have a son and daughter with PhDs, in the tradition of Sue's siblings and other children who collected an astonishing number of college degrees after growing up on and around those plantations.

## *Chapter 23*

# Lyman Johnson

Long before Tayshaun Price, John Wall, Anthony Davis and other African American athletic stars at the University of Kentucky, there was Lyman Johnson.

Johnson was also a man of color, but he was a Louisville high school history teacher, not an athlete when he became the first black person officially admitted as a student at UK. This was in 1949 when Kentucky schools and colleges were still segregated. Johnson broke the color barrier by winning a court order from a federal judge in Lexington.

When black players were finally recruited for basketball and football teams, UK was lagging behind other South Eastern Conference (SEC) schools, but it has caught up, with no apparent loss of fans, especially for its national championship basketball teams.

Lyman Johnson was Kentucky's leading crusader for equity in the twentieth century. When admitted to UK, he already had a degree from the University of Michigan, where he found himself in all-white classes.

To him, "equal" meant blacks and whites together—in schools, housing, at play, on the buses, at work and in the voting precincts. One early battle was against the Louisville Free Public Library, which excluded blacks. "It was neither free nor public," he said.

Growing up in Tennessee, one of nine children of a principal of a black school, Johnson had a long memory for racial oppression. His grandparents had been slaves.

Lyman Johnson (right) with Rufus Atwood, president of Kentucky State (now Kentucky State University), at door of U.S. District Court after winning admission to the UK graduate program in history in 1949. *Courtesy of Lexington* Herald-Leader.

In Louisville, he was always on his feet in class after spending many nights organizing blacks to fight for their rights.

"I didn't want my enemies to catch me dozing at my desk," he told me in a KET interview. "I was a stand-up teacher!"

By the time of his death at ninety-one, in October 1997, Louisville had named a school for him and elected him to the school board. The University of Kentucky gave him an honorary doctorate. The state's leaders recognized that the "stand-up" teacher was a Kentuckian of vision and courage.

## Chapter 24

# A Black Woman's Story

*July 1, 1995*

Georgia Davis Powers is an important figure in Kentucky history. She was the first woman and the first African American elected to the state Senate. She won five terms, chaired two major committees and effectively championed the causes of blacks, women, children, the poor and the handicapped.

Her impressive achievements in legislative politics and the struggle for racial justice deserved a book, and now we have it—not just a recounting of what laws were passed or color barriers broken, her public life, but also the private life.

The private life, she says, included an affair with the Reverend Dr. Martin Luther King in the year leading up to King's death. Indeed, they were together in a Memphis motel the night before King was gunned down on the balcony there in April 1968.

Powers' decision to write about King as her lover became a national news headline when the book was published, but the exploitive aspects—the publisher's choice of a title and gaudy jacket with King in the foreground and Powers in the background—may have lost her two kinds of readers: blacks who are offended by references to King's infidelities and literate whites and blacks who mistake this for another sleep-and-tell story.

The book also received a rough reception from columnists in the state's two largest newspapers. Betty Winston Baye in the *Courier-Journal* and Art

Georgia Davis Powers was the first black woman to serve in the Kentucky State Senate and did so with distinction. She served more than twenty years, focusing on civil rights and open housing laws. *Courtesy of Kentucky Legislative Research Commission.*

Jester in the *Lexington Herald-Leader* thought that the author's emphasis on her romance with King diverted attention from her own role and the "lifting up" of other "movement women" in the civil rights era (Baye) and "plays to the voyeurism and sensationalism of our own time" (Jester). In sum, they seem to ask: Why did this prominent Kentucky woman give us all this detail?

Well, why not? First, the book is not really about King; it is about Powers, born in 1923, the only daughter in a family of nine children whose parents moved to Louisville when the two-room shack they called home in Washington County blew away in a 1925 tornado. It is about growing up in a segregated city with a father, Ben Montgomery, who worked for forty-two years at a Louisville factory and who fed not only his large family in the Depression, but also shared food from a relative's farm with neighbors who had none. Montgomery's father was white, but Georgia's grandmother never told his name. And when Georgia was fifteen and raped by a man they all knew, she never told her parents.

Details about King? Yes, but also other men—a first lover who betrayed her by having a baby with another woman; a first husband who broke a promise to help her go to college.

And others: ministers—one who tried to seduce her on the day of her baptism, and those with whom she put her life on the line in demonstrations at Selma, Montgomery, St. Petersburg, Memphis and Frankfort. Louisville politicians, notably Raoul Cunningham, who was black, and Norbert Blume, who was white, helped her win that Senate seat in 1967. White senators like Mike Moloney, David Karem and Kelsey Friend helped her keep the office by teaching her how to use it.

More details: working across the country in wartime jobs, as a riveter, a telephone operator and data processor—more than thirty-two jobs by the time she got into state politics "as a token black" in the Wilson Wyatt senate race in 1962. There she met Lucretia Ward, an East End white woman who became her closest friend as the two of them helped organize the 1964 march on Frankfort for a public accommodations law. This was when Georgia Powers met King, but it was three years later, she says, when their friendship turned to intimacy.

"Why am I telling all of this now?" she writes. "If Dr. King had been an ordinary man, the telling of my story wouldn't have made much difference. However, Dr. King was no ordinary man. His life will be studied by scholars long after I am gone…I want the part relating to me to be available in my own words. It is my own history as well, both the good and the bad."

Georgia Powers was no ordinary woman. In her first bid for office, she was opposed by the regular Democratic organization and by members of her own race controlled by the regulars. In Jefferson County politics and for a while in the Senate, she fought the Good Old Boys club. Always, there were two strikes against her: her race and her sex. She triumphed anyway.

Forget the publicity and hype, the criticism of this book, and read it with an open mind for the honest memoir, the incredibly valuable piece of first-person history that it really is. You will be overcome.

## Chapter 25

# Atticus in Alabama

*January 21, 2007*

For those of us who were children when the South was rigidly segregated, Harper Lee's novel *To Kill a Mockingbird* is the story of the region when we were young. Seen through the eyes of the precocious daughter of a white lawyer who fights to save the life of an unjustly accused black man, it is a child's perspective on the central issue of American history: race and equal rights.

The black man loses the trial and his life; the white child and her brother are almost killed. But in the telling of these events, Lee created a literary classic that may be as important to the history of civil rights as Harriet Beecher Stowe's *Uncle Tom's Cabin* was to the Civil War.

A little over a week ago, I flew to Birmingham, Alabama, to join my daughter Catherine McCarty, her husband and their younger son on a trip to Montgomery to see a highly acclaimed high school performance of a stage version of Lee's book.

My older grandson, Connor McCarty, sixteen, was playing Boo Radley, the lawyer's mentally troubled neighbor, in the multiracial cast of sixty kids from two Birmingham area high schools.

The Montgomery performance was an encore of the show that had won national attention in October because it was a combined effort of students and teachers from schools separated by a sharp economic and cultural divide.

In Montgomery, Lee, now eighty, was a guest of honor along with Douglas Jones, the white prosecutor who in 2001 convicted one of the four original suspects in the 1963 bombing deaths of four black girls at a Birmingham church. Jones was only nine at the time of the bombing, one of the most horrific attacks of the civil rights era.

Lee, who rarely appears or speaks in public, met with the students at a private reception after the play. My grandson was so overcome with emotion that he burst into tears as she shook his hand. And then, to our surprise, she entered a public area adjacent to the theater where a line of appreciative fans quickly formed to meet her.

When she learned I was from Lexington, she gave me a warm smile and a message to "tell Reed Polk hello for me."

Polk is the widely known former minister and hospital executive who was a childhood friend of Lee's in Monroeville, Alabama. Many Lexington schoolchildren have enjoyed his oft-told and moving account of a Christmas parade in Monroeville in 1957 that he witnessed with Lee.

Because the parade was to feature the first integration of the black and white school bands, Ku Klux Klan members turned out to disrupt it. But the business community and the police resisted, and the protest failed.

"Reed, you would never believe what I am doing," Lee told him in an encounter at the parade, "I'm writing a novel."

"What about?" asked Polk, who was home from his first year in college.

Waving an arm toward the street, the bands, the crowds, the police and the Klan members, she replied, "Oh, all of this."

Also in the reception line to meet Lee was Wade Hall, who wrote some twenty books about Kentucky and the South when he was a professor at Bellarmine College in Louisville.

Now living in retirement at his birthplace near Montgomery, Hall pressed an earlier request that Lee give a lecture that he has endowed at Troy University near his home.

"I'll come and get you," Hall said, "drive you to Troy and back to Monroeville the same day."

"Why Professor Hall, I'd be dead by nightfall," she replied.

"This is the most gracious turn down I've ever received," he sighed.

Lee's book was published in 1960, seven years after I turned down an offer from the *Birmingham News* to leave the *Times-Picayune* in New Orleans, where I was a police reporter. The *News* wanted me to take on the same job in Birmingham because it was having trouble with the city's notorious police commissioner "Bull" Connor and heard I was a rather bold reporter.

Gregory Peck as Atticus Finch in the movie *To Kill a Mockingbird.*

At the time, I was married to a Birmingham girl who was a distant cousin of Georgia's U.S. senator Richard Russell, a staunch segregationist. She, however, was a campus radical at Tulane.

By the time Lee told Polk she was writing a book, which Hall says is "really about power, the power the whites held and didn't want to surrender," I was divorced and had just been fired because of a drunken argument in New Orleans.

While on my new job as a reporter for a weekly paper in Russellville, Kentucky, in January 1958, I saw a high school basketball game with black and white players on each team, a first for me.

Times were changing in Kentucky, but Alabama clung to massive resistance. By 1963, I was sober, but that was the year the Klan bombed the Sixteenth Street church, Connor turned the police dogs on black demonstrators and President John F. Kennedy was assassinated.

Would I have survived in Lee's Alabama a half century ago? Probably not.

But I am glad there were those who did and who paid the price to bring together white and black children in a play that, to quote Atticus Finch, is not about "the white race or the black race. This is about the human race."

And that's what I told Jones, the prosecutor, when we shook hands in Montgomery. Then I thought: He is Atticus.

# Part VIII

# *Politics*

*Chapter 26*

# Shooting Straight on Sin

*August 7, 1998*

Having practiced as a volunteer chaplain for wayward Washington Democrats by successfully counseling his friend Senator Ted Kennedy to get a new life, Senator Orrin Hatch, Republican from Utah and a Mormon, advises President Clinton, Southern Baptist, to go for confession and forgiveness. Although the White House seems to be sticking to its "didn't happen" story, Hatch's call for Mr. Clinton to "pour his heart out" about the Monica Lewinsky affair points to a path out that has worked for other political leaders.

In the presidential campaign of 1884, the Republican press exploited a story that Democratic candidate Grover Cleveland had fathered an illegitimate son. With cartoons of a baby screaming, "Ma, Ma, where's my Pa?" and the answer, "Gone to the White House, Ha! Ha! Ha!" Cleveland, a bachelor who was governor of New York, told his frantic advisors "Tell the truth."

Cleveland may indeed have been the father, but by acknowledging the facts forthrightly, "he pulled the stinger" out of the scandal, says Kentucky's historian laureate, Thomas D. Clark. After the voters learned the whole story, they elected Cleveland to not one but two terms.

In the same Victorian era, five-term Kentucky congressman, William C.P. Breckinridge of Lexington lost his brilliant political career in a scandal over his spurned mistress and a breach-of-promise lawsuit that was the talk of the nation. But his admissions about the affair, which began when she was seventeen and he a married man of forty-seven, helped win back so many friends that he was defeated by only the narrowest of margins, 255 votes, in 1894.

As historian James Kotter tells the story in his book *The Breckinridges of Kentucky, 1760–1981,* "Willie" Breckinridge, acclaimed as the best orator in Congress and perhaps a future speaker of the House of Representatives, began the road to redemption on the witness stand in a Washington courtroom:

"She was a woman of passion. I was a man of passion. We yielded ourselves to each other. That was all."

It was unforgettable theater, but not enough. The jury gave his former lover $15,000, three years of a congressman's salary in that day. Waves of denunciation rolled across the United States, from pulpit, press and political platform, none more intense than in Breckinridge's hometown, but he sought reelection anyway.

On May 4, 1894, at the Lexington Opera House, before an almost totally male audience, many as openly hostile as nearly every woman in the city, Breckinridge, former Confederate colonel, eloquent spokesman for progressive causes, supporter of women's rights, defender of oppressed blacks and a disgraced hero, made the second dramatic admission in his comeback.

After recounting his career in the House, his past elections and his national standing in the party, he told them what they came to hear:

"I knew the secret sin; I tried to atone for it" but "entangled by weakness, by passion, by sin, in coils which it was almost impossible to break," he had failed. If there were men better qualified let them be chosen. Select "someone whose life has been stainless," he declaimed, "whose nights have been stainless, whose ability is ample and whose experience is wide. For a hundred years, this district has been represented by men. They have not always been sinless men." He stood back and brushed away a tear.

The effect was magnetic, Klotter writes. "In the bold and almost arrogant speech, the old eloquence still remained and won victories. His audience was completely at his command, wild with enthusiasms and ready apparently to rend his accusers. Many who had come to scoff remained to pray."

Three months later, riding to a speech in Athens, Kentucky, Breckinridge was escorted by 180 cavalrymen riding two abreast while 350 "rebels" proceeded on foot in column formation. He was defiant as well as contrite, with his band sometimes ending a rally by striking up the provocative air, "The Girl I Left Behind Me." There were opponents everywhere, including one thousand women at a protest rally, and in the biggest turnout ever recorded in a primary in the district, they prevailed, but only by less than 1 percent of the vote.

Cleveland was a dull, unimaginative but principled man remembered by the presidential historians as "near great." He had an enjoyable and honored retirement living in Princeton, New Jersey. Breckinridge, more gifted than almost any citizen of his generation in Kentucky, lived out his days in Lexington with people who knew all about him, the good and the bad. He became an enormously influential writer of editorials for his son's newspaper, the *Herald*, expressing an optimistic and progressive view about the future.

When he died in 1904, it was said the funeral attendance was the second largest in Lexington history, exceeded only by the mourners for Henry Clay in 1852.

A century later, snared in a similar web of public allegations about a political leader's private sex life, Mr. Clinton has heard the altar call that Cleveland and Breckinridge heard. The truth set them free. Why not Clinton? Hatch is right.

Clinton did admit the affair with Lewinsky, after first denying it, and made amends, of sorts, to his wife Hilary, in his support of her political career.

A decade or so later, Secretary of State Hillary Clinton was one of the world's most admired women in public polls. The former president, with the popularity of a rock star in his own very public private life, was chosen as a marquee speaker for the 2012 Democratic convention.

Not so fortunate was North Carolina's former U.S. senator John Edwards, his own career in shambles over an affair he tried to hide as a presidential aspirant while his once supportive wife was battling the cancer that killed her.

## Chapter 27

# "Getting" Happy

Truly a "political legend" in his own time, and not shy to admit it—flexing an arm in old age to demonstrate vigor and inviting admirers to "feel that muscle, pardner"—Albert Benjamin "Happy" Chandler won two terms as governor and a U.S. Senate seat. He was honored as the National Baseball Commissioner who permitted Dodgers owner Branch Rickey to integrate the game with Jackie Robinson. He even attended a national Democratic convention as a potential nominee for president.

This was all before we became friends over a series of colorful interviews we did together on KET in 1975.

Certainly the leading cheerleader of his own fan club, he refused to rate his two terms as governor (1935–39 and 1955–59)—"they were equally good, Albert Benjamin." (Although my first name is Albert, the middle name is not "Benjamin"; that was his, but he often tacked it on mine, I think, because he liked to hear the sound of his own name.)

Dismissive of many other governors, he especially scorned the much admired Bert Combs from the mountains (whom he called "the little judge") whose hand-picked successor Edward T. "Ned" Breathitt defeated Happy's bid for an unprecedented third term as governor in 1963. About the Merit System created by Combs and Breathitt, Chandler fulminated on TV: "It is a fraud, Albert Benjamin."

In Logan County, when I arrived to edit the paper, many old-timers demonized Happy for his 1935 victory in a race for governor over Thomas Rhea of Russellville, a kingpin of Democratic Party politics. But after

A.B. "Happy" Chandler in late life. *Courtesy of UK Special Collections.*

researching the record and allegations that the Rhea machine turned out more voters than were registered on the books that year, I began to "get" a different picture of Chandler.

Historians praise his reorganization of state government and other improvements in his first term.

Although given to boasts about his Confederate ancestry and politically unacceptable language about blacks when they were not around, he stood tall for civil rights in his second term. He sent tanks and three thousand National Guardsmen to his native western Kentucky to enforce school integration in resistant communities.

On TV, he told me, as he famously said many times, that the case for admitting Jackie Robinson to the Major Leagues came down to a vision of the hereafter.

"I said, 'When my maker asks me, "Why didn't you let this fellow play?"' and I answer, 'He was black,' he's going to say, 'I don't think that's good enough!'"

When Martha Helen and I were running the newspaper in London, Kentucky in the 1980s, Happy's grandson Ben, then a college student, would chauffeur him to London and leave him at the Ramada Inn restaurant on I-75, like a Pony Express package. Happy, who didn't drive, would await the arrival of a friend, Joe Weddington of Prestonsburg, to drive him on to Atlanta. There he would join another former governor, Ellis Arnall of Georgia, for meetings of an insurance company board on which they served. Weddington was always late for the pickup, so Happy would call the newspaper office and command me and Martha Helen to join him for lunch, which we did.

When Weddington finally arrived, usually two hours late, and reached for a menu, the old governor would interrupt and say, "I've had my lunch! Let's go!" Of course, the tardy Weddington always left the Ramada hungry.

About Weddington, his devoted disciple, Happy commented, "On Judgment Day when the Good Lord orders all who want to join him in Heaven to come forth, Joe Weddington will come fifth!"

When Happy died at ninety-two in June 1991, politicians, sports figures and journalists used a lot of words about his long public career. I went out to Versailles to his famous backyard log cabin, really a lodge in the presidential Camp David style, for interviews by the TV stations. After his grandsons and I swapped color stories for the cameras, I returned home and wrote my own tribute for the Lexington paper.

It was my conclusion that a young woman unable to speak a eulogy might well represent the best of Chandler's service to Kentucky.

This was the nineteen-year-old who had received a lung transplant at the Albert B. Chandler Medical Center at UK the same weekend that Happy died.

A surgeon employed that year to run the Chandler Center's heart and lung transplant program operated on the young woman. In March he had performed the new program's first heart transplant. Looking back on those KET shows with me in 1975, I was glad I cited the creation of a second state-supported medical school as the landmark accomplishment in his second term in the 1950's.

Many governors rearrange the way the state does business, but few start a medical school.

This was an issue in his 1955 campaign when opposition came from supporters of the existing medical school at the University of Louisville. The argument that prevailed, however, was the need for a UK-based school to meet the needs of rural Kentuckians. More than a third of Kentuckians lived in counties where there was but one doctor for every 2,314 people, Chandler pointed out. In 1964, after years of bitter controversy, the new UK College of Medicine conferred degrees on its first thirty-two graduates.

Nearly fifty years later, as this book was going to press, a $1 billion renovation and expansion was nearly completed at the Chandler center.

None of this would have been possible without the political process in which Happy was the leader. It's one of the reasons they invited him to sing "My Old Kentucky Home" at all those UK games. In a state with so many health problems, his enduring legacy was doctors trained, illness treated and lives saved at that hospital.

## Chapter 28

# Why Clements and Prichard Still Matter

*October 21, 2009*

When I invited my wife to join me this week for a history program on President Lyndon Johnson, I noted that the speakers were Bess and Tyler Abell, the daughter and son-in-law of the late Kentucky governor and senator, Earle C. Clements, who was LBJ's great friend, and Bobby Baker, LBJ's onetime indispensible go-to aide in the US Senate.

"I'm busy," my wife replied. "You go. I thought those people were in a museum."

Despite my bruised feelings (the panelists were younger than I), I took a front row seat at the Young Library at University of Kentucky for an event called the "Prichard Lecture," named for the whiz kid lawyer from Bourbon County, Princeton and Harvard who dazzled Washington with his smarts in the 1940s, then returned home with plans to become governor, maybe president, but went to jail instead, over a ballot stuffing scandal. Sometimes we can be *too* smart.

For all his brilliant promise, Prichard endured incredible humiliation for his stupidity, but when he died in 1984, the funeral was attended by leaders from Washington and Frankfort and friends across Kentucky. He had fallen "short of the glory," as his biographer Tracy Campbell writes, but his redemption was acknowledged in the progressive causes he championed after he emerged from prison. Even in disgrace he was too brilliant to be ignored by Democratic governors who sought his advice and skills in moving Kentucky forward in the 1960s and 70s.

Edward F. Prichard Jr. was blind and suffering from diabetes when leading the Prichard Committee for Academic Excellence. Robert Sexton (right) was the committee's only executive director until his death in 2010. *Courtesy of the Prichard Committee for Academic Excellence.*

Although the Abells and Baker talked a little about their assigned topic, an inside account of Kentucky and LBJ's White House, where the Abells both worked, they mostly focused on LBJ's problems and personality. They didn't mention LBJ's friend Prichard. But old-timers from state political wars knew that Prichard was a protégé of Earle Clements, Kentucky's "first modern governor," as Bess Abell described him, and Clements was an innovative "liberal" (no better word for it) who marched us out of the nineteenth century. Clements influenced Prichard's generation as he built parks, roads and other infrastructure, funded schools, reorganized the state police, and struggled to end segregation and control the coal industry.

Clements, one of LBJ's closest friends as a fellow senator, was a pivotal figure in Johnson's path to power. His loyalty as acting majority leader when LBJ was stricken with a heart attack in 1955 distracted Clements from his own reelection campaign. He lost the race to Republican Thruston Morton the next year. The impact of that loss on Kentucky is almost incalculable. Were Clements still in the Senate when LBJ became vice president and president, historian Jim Klotter says, there's little doubt he would have become majority leader, gaining the influence with which Alben Barkley before him showered Kentucky with federal benefits in President Franklin D. Roosevelt's New Deal.

As it was, when Clements died at eighty-eight in Morganfield, his importance in Kentucky history had become obscured by the colorful claims of his longtime party rival A.B. "Happy" Chandler, some of which were true, and importantly so, but Clements's legacy matters. So does that of Prichard who died in 1984, at sixty-nine, the memories of his fall and comeback fading except in Campbell's book and the activist Prichard Committee for Academic Excellence.

Despite their defects (Clements was cold and unforgiving, Prichard overly infatuated with his own biting wit, and not careful about debt), they mastered politics at the grass roots. Before he became governor and senator, Clements held elective offices at the courthouse, statehouse and congressional level. Prichard knew every legislator in Frankfort and officials in 120 counties before he finished college. They quickly gained access to power in Washington, Clements with LBJ, Prichard with FDR, because they knew how. Their rural roots were an asset, not a liability. They sensed that Washington was like an outsized Kentucky courthouse, the struggle for resources, a mirror of small courthouse conflicts over favors—"who gets the rock?"

In a state like Kentucky, leadership often falls to political hacks or fresh faces with painless promises, which fail. Clements and Prichard mattered because they knew the game before they got on the field and played it courageously, with a vision that had lasting, positive consequences. Where is the courage, where is the vision for Kentucky today?

# Chapter 29

# Before Mitch

Mitch McConnell, leader of the Republican Party in the U.S. Senate in the early years of a new century, is a very smart man. Clearly his seniority and rank among his peers reflect a keen understanding of what works to gain power and hold it. There is more to know about polling, fundraising and influencing public attitudes than any of McConnell's Republican predecessors from Kentucky had mastered when they were mentoring him. But he "got" the drift toward the new technology of politics in 1984 when he upset incumbent Walter "Dee" Huddleston, a likeable Democrat, with a series of "hound dog" TV ads depicting Dee as an absentee senator.

Later, when Bill Clinton was president and I was unable to persuade any prominent Democrats to join me on a radio talk show about the case for Clinton's campaign for the North American Fair Trade Agreement (NAFTA), it was Mitch who came on with a forthright expression of support. In a state where there was much anxiety about free trade, this was a moment of courage, I concluded.

In recent years, appalled by increasing partisan gridlock in Washington, I have been troubled by our senior senator's rightward tilt to maintain his party leadership. With nothing I can do about it, however, I will share just a few memories of the Republican senators who were his friends, and mine, none of them very doctrinaire, when he and I were younger. My point is to recall their independence when they voted their conscience rather than the party line. Those senators were John Sherman Cooper of Somerset, and Thruston Morton and Marlow Cook of Louisville.

Cooper served three partial terms as senator and two full terms. He was ambassador, first to India and then to East Germany. He opposed the war in Vietnam and, together with Frank Church, a Democrat from Idaho, introduced the Cooper-Church Amendment, an effort to restrict the deployment of troops during a war against the wishes of the president. The amendment passed in the Senate after a long filibuster and six months of debate, but failed in the House of Representatives. Nevertheless, the effort showed Cooper's ability to work in a bipartisan manner. And he never concealed his personal friendship with President John Kennedy and his brother Edward.

Thruston Morton, who was chairman of the National Republican Party, 1959–61, voted for the Civil Rights Act in 1964. Deeply troubled by the Vietnam War, he left the senate in 1968. In an interview for KET, he told me he regretted the exaggerated partisan language he used in beating back a challenge for his seat from fellow Louisville lawyer and one-time friend Wilson Wyatt.

In Marlow Cook's one term in the senate, he became a close friend of Democrat Huddleston and was one of the Republicans who early called for Richard Nixon to resign the presidency in the Watergate scandal. Earlier, in the Kentucky legislature, rooming with a fellow lawmaker, Tom Ray, a Democrat, also from Louisville, Cook co-sponsored with Ray a bill creating Kentucky Educational Television network (KET).

In retirement in Sarasota, Florida, where he has been a popular civic leader, Cook has endorsed local taxes for education, the environment and roads. In a heavily Republican county of conservative older residents, those tax measures have all passed.

Here are my favorite stories about each of these former senators.

About Thruston Morton: When his staff questioned his French cuffs, with gold links, and black limousine as he campaigned in the mountains of Eastern Kentucky, he rebuffed them. "They have already elected me once; they know I am a U.S. Senator. They want and expect me to *look* like a senator and that's who I am."

About Marlow Cook: When Bill Clinton ran against George H.W. Bush, Cook was heard to say, "With a wife and all my daughters, I am voting for Bill Clinton even though I'm a Republican. None of my women folks would expect me to support a president who is not for choice."

About John Sherman Cooper: Rejecting staff recommendations to put out a whispering campaign against an opponent known to them as a womanizer, Cooper told them "Well, folks, there's a considerable slippin' around vote out there—we don't want to lose it."

So, it's another time, but I miss those men. Perhaps it was the war in which we all served. We knew we couldn't win it by ourselves. We had to help each other.

## *Chapter 30*

# "Teacher Men"

When Kentucky's system of higher education began to change in the 1960s, the conversion of former teacher colleges to regional universities was led by educator politicians. Two of them, Robert R. Martin and Adron Doran, began their careers as what old timers used to call "teacher men" and then into politics by which they earned appointments respectively as presidents of the colleges that became Eastern Kentucky and Morehead State Universities.

A third leader, Kelly Thompson, was a popular public relations director at Western Kentucky in Bowling Green who became interim president when the incumbent died suddenly in 1955. He was such a promotional wizard that he held the post over a period of phenomenal growth for the next fourteen years and then ran a school foundation until his death at eighty-four in 1993.

Martin and Doran traveled the classic road from Depression-era rural poverty to classroom teaching and then out and up to statewide prominence. Martin, a burly man in an almost white raincoat, was running Bert Combs's second, and this time successful, campaign for governor the rainy fall night in 1959 when I met him over a hamburger steak supper at the Harvest Inn in Elkton, one town over from Russellville. Our companions were two other gents in identical raincoats, the silver-haired Combs and my new friend who brought me along, Emerson "Doc" Beauchamp, the cunning Democratic chieftain of Logan County–this was the era when we were often accused after lopsided elections, "but never trapped," a *Courier-Journal* columnist wrote.

Combs's subsequent victory over an opponent backed by Governor Happy Chandler won Martin his college presidency and started him on the success he achieved in educational "empire building" along with his rivals Thompson and Doran.

All three skillfully organized regional coalitions to lobby funding for their campuses, usually at the expense of the University of Kentucky. When Martin died in 1997, Otis Singletary, the former UK president, and I were driven to the funeral in Richmond by Terry Birdwhistell, later dean of libraries at UK. When we stopped on the way for breakfast, Singletary recalled a friendly welcome to Kentucky from Martin and Doran at his first meeting of the Council on Higher Education. "They took me around the table as the newest guy in the room and introduced me to all the trustees. They could not have been more cordial," said Singletary.

"Then, when the meeting started, Doran made a motion to separate all the community colleges from UK and Martin seconded it!" That motion failed; the separation of the colleges didn't happen until the next century rolled around. Still, when we arrived at the church Singletary declined an invitation to sit near the front row. "I'm afraid they will think I'm trying to make sure Bob is really dead," he whispered.

Although Doran is remembered for expanding Morehead in the mountains, his political career began as a state legislator from western Kentucky. He was also a preacher in the Church of Christ and speaker of the House when he sought the presidency of a college, Murray State near his home county of Graves. Fearful of giving so much influence to a man they suspected of ambitions to be governor, the state's "king makers" made him settle for Morehead, then with only seven hundred students far away from his base. Undaunted, he organized the Morehead region for Combs's chosen successor Edward Breathitt in his race against Happy and that generated millions to grow the enrollment ten-fold after Breathitt won.

In my youth, I scoffed at those "teacher men" as despots, for, indeed, they ran their schools as fiefdoms with little tolerance for academic or student independence. But as I aged, I acknowledged that there was some merit to treating the campus community as "family." Never rejecting an invitation to speak for commencement at a high school, no matter how small, always reassuring poor anxious parents they would find financial aid for their children and protect them from harm, they created a new middle class in this state—from a great wave of young Kentuckians, most of whom were the first in their families to get a college education.

In retirement, Doran and I bonded a bit, united by mutual friendships with two younger men of politics, Terry McBrayer, a Democrat, and Larry Forgy, a Republican, who each ran but lost races for governor. Forgy served with Doran on a bank board in Morehead. McBrayer, a Morehead graduate who was treated like a son by the childless Doran and his wife, Mignon, told me Adron secured a law school scholarship for him at the University of Louisville when there wasn't one by taking him to the president's office and begging until President Phillip Davidson gave in.

Although the Church of Christ, the church of my youth, has only ministers and elders as leaders, I used to tease Doran and call him "the bishop." When he was a frail old man sipping the soup Martha Helen and I had brought to him and Mignon at their retirement apartment in Lexington, he noted that I had become an Episcopalian and another friend, Mike Adams, the Centre College president who later was president of University of Georgia, had also defected from Doran's church to another denomination. In this, our last visit before he died, he worriedly shook his head and mused, "Al, you and Mike know so much. How did you both go so wrong?"

*Chapter 31*

# Nunn and Ned

When John Sherman Cooper died in Washington in 1991, I flew to Washington for his funeral at Arlington with my friend Lois Gray, former governor Louie Nunn, and two of Lois's sons, Jim and Stephen Gray.

Politically, the Grays were Democrats, but back in the day when they all lived in Glasgow and Louie was the Republican judge executive of Barren County, he was their lawyer. When Louie was learning politics under Senator Cooper's tutelage, Lois's father, the politically influential country doctor, C.C. Howard, a Democrat, was crusading to eradicate tuberculosis in Kentucky. The Grays and Nunns became friends who knew how to "reach out" to the other side. This was especially useful to Nunn as governor when he won over enough Democrats in the legislature to pass a two-cent increase in the sales tax.

After checking in at our Washington hotel the night before the funeral, we were joined for dinner by former governor Edward T. "Ned" Breathitt, Jody Powell, President Jimmy Carter's press secretary who had become a lobbyist, and my friend Rudy Abramson, a Washington reporter for the *Los Angeles Times*. It was a treat to hear amusing recollections from the two governors about their campaigns in the sixties, their race against each other, when Ned defeated Louie for governor by thirteen thousand votes in 1963, and Louie's victory in the next governor's race over Ned's endorsed candidate Henry Ward, by twenty-eight thousand votes.

Nunn and Breathitt became close after Governor Martha Layne Collins (1963–67) recruited them to work together, successively, as trustees at two different state universities in need of seasoned guidance to resolve vexing controversies.

Former governors Louie Nunn and Edward T. Breathitt Jr., on the KET set, made appearances together to support educational programs after Governor Martha Layne Collins called on them for assistance in the 1980s. *Courtesy of KET.*

Twelve years later, when Breathitt died at seventy-eight, I invited Nunn to be a guest on my *Comment on Kentucky* tribute. Other guests were Lois Combs Weinberg, Governor Combs's daughter, Don Mills, who was Breathitt's former press secretary, and journalist John Ed Pearce, whose critical columns about Nunn eased after the sales tax increase, which Pearce favored. Pearce believed, as did I, that, despite Nunn's jingoistic support of the Vietnam War and showy dispatch of the National Guard to the UK campus during a student protest, the sales tax hike to support programs enacted by Combs and Breathitt placed Nunn in the ranks of progressive governors.

Accepting my invitation for the Breathitt tribute, Nunn cancelled a fundraising speech for Republican candidates but asked to be seated on the TV set between Pearce and Mills. In the dressing room at KET, he explained to them that he made the request "in hopes of a Christ-like feeling." We all laughed but later were moved by Nunn's last words on the show, eulogizing his former foe turned friend as "one of the finest gentlemen I have ever known." Three months later, on January 29, 2004, Nunn also died, at seventy-nine.

As "the game" of politics becomes more like war in an era of fast-changing technology, I have increasingly fond memories of Louie Nunn's zest for down-home politics and the apt humorous remark about what was going on. When I told him his former budget officer Larry Forgy seemed to find fund raising in his own race for governor "distasteful," Louie snorted, "Well, if something is distasteful, don't put it in your mouth!"

Joining a student body audience at Centre College to hear me lecture on "the old politics," he guffawed at my memory of Speaker Sam Rayburn's comment on President Kennedy's cabinet full of Harvard graduates: "I'd like it better if just one of them fellows had ever run for sheriff."

When I called on Louie to tell the students his take on the comment of a later U.S. House speaker, Tip O'Neill, that "all politics is local," he recalled a visit he made as governor to a judge executive at Columbia in rural Adair County.

"It was during another Cold War crisis with the Russians," Nunn said, "but of course I was there to talk about a county road."

On the way into the courthouse, however, he was surprised when an old guy in overalls sitting on a bench outside and whittling at a stick, called to him, "Governor, are ye going to protect us from them Commies?"

"What's the matter?" Nunn replied. "You afraid they're going to nuke the Courthouse?"

The old fellow spit out a chew of tobacco juice. "It's the county seat, ain't it?"

*Chapter 32*

# Tea Party

## A review of *The Tea Party: A Brief History*, Ronald Formisano

*June 17, 2012*

A University of Kentucky professor once told me that to understand the roots of populist discontent in our state I should read a term paper written by Edward F. Prichard Jr. in 1935 when he was a twenty-year-old senior from Paris, Kentucky, at Princeton University.

Entitled "Popular Political Movements in Kentucky, 1875–1900," this undergraduate research of 256 pages was the equivalent of a PhD dissertation, the professor said.

Reading this paper, an analysis of Democratic and Republican politics after Reconstruction and the third-party impulses at the fringes of the two parties, I was struck by young Prichard's sympathies for the farmers, miners and workers who owned no property whom he saw as both frustrated independent actors and "a pitiful object of corruption in elections."

Now, with Prichard, who died in 1984, more remembered as the redeemed champion of education reform in his last years than for the achievements and mistakes of the brilliant but arrogant political activist he was in his youth, another UK professor has written a study of the political eruption that has roiled the nation and Kentucky's politics since 2009.

A timely primer on the subject that most dominated the news of this week's primary elections, *The Tea Party: A Brief History*, by Ronald Formisano, provides basic information about its origins, its significance and its place in political history

Brief, indeed, one could have read most of this book between the closing of the polls Tuesday and final tallies on KET that showed Thomas Massie, the boyish Lewis County judge executive with the MIT degree and endorsement of U.S. Senator Rand Paul, had romped over two well-established Republicans to win the nomination for an open congressional seat in Kentucky's Fourth District.

Having finished the book by bedtime, a reader might marvel at Formisano's report that the Tea Party movement (TEA as in "taxed enough already") and supporters "now virtually dominate the Republican base and in 2012 may constitute 40 percent of Republican voters." Although Paul is one of four senators who caucus as Tea Party members, he and his look-like protégé Massie ran as Republicans. Amazingly, however, polls show 10 percent of all voters in the party regard themselves as Tea Party members first and Republicans second. "About half of all Tea Party activists hold an unfavorable view of the Republican party," Formisano writes.

Tea Party public protests didn't emerge until after the George W. Bush administration had left office, but once President Obama entered the Oval Office, Tea Party rallies and marches "focused like a laser beam" on their core issues: federal government spending, the soaring debt and big government.

The social insurgencies of the late nineteenth century studied by Ed Prichard created a populist clamor for cheaper money, debt relief, reduced working hours, an end to child labor and protection for unions that could only come through more, rather than less, government regulation. The Progressive Era (1908–1924) saw an activist government break-up of the monied trusts, but, paradoxically, many of today's Tea Party members, viewing government as "the enemy," support their campaigns with rivers of cash from wealthy anti-tax donors who are not, perhaps, all that different from the railroad and Wall Street "robber barons" who were seen as "the special interests" one hundred years ago.

An occasional contributor of opinion articles of a liberal perspective to the *Lexington Herald-Leader*, Formisano is a respected authority on the history of populist movements. In an even-handed way he writes of the origins of the Tea Party or Tea Parties (there are many competing factions), in resentments against so-called "elites" and various alliances and rejections at the grass roots. Seven short chapters give insights on involvements by the religious right and big business, mad-as-hell frustration with politics as usual, media coverage (especially by a supportive Fox News) and "Astroturf populism," described by the much demonized Democratic leader Nancy Pelosi as a movement more artificial than authentic by some of the wealthiest Americans "to keep the focus on tax cuts for the rich instead of for the great middle class."

## *Chapter 33*

# Reforming Gatewood

*January 15, 2012*

Gatewood Galbraith's untimely death from pneumonia this week produced such an impressive outpouring of admiration from political leaders he opposed and journalists who never endorsed him in his five races for governor that I have been overcome with remorse for my efforts to reform him.

What on earth was I thinking? It was over lunch at Ramsey's on High Street in Lexington (a symbolic thoroughfare on which to pitch a lifestyle change to Kentucky's best known advocate of legalized marijuana) that I told Gate it was time to straighten up and go on the lecture circuit.

This was back in the '80s or '90s (does it matter?) when he had stumbled once more at the finish line but left the whole state laughing over one of his humorous campaigns.

At Owensboro, Republican Larry Forgy later told me, Gatewood was sitting between him and Democrat Brereton Jones at a lunch for governor candidates of both parties. The audience was huge. Suddenly Gatewood jostled Forgy and Jones as he speared a dinner roll and began to butter it.

"Look at that crowd, Forgy," he mused. Then, turning to Jones, "Brery—I bet I'm the only sonovabitch here who came for the meal!"

Fast-forwarding to the post-election lunch at Ramsey's, I guess I was seized with the zeal of a recovering alcoholic who wants to dry up everybody else. "Gatewood, you need a different public life," I said sternly. "Give up these silly races; get an agent to book you for speeches on the college campuses.

Perhaps the state's best known failed candidate for office in modern times, Gatewood Galbraith was a maverick who became popular for his wit and candor. *Courtesy of KET.*

You will drive those kids crazy with your jokes, make a lot of money and then you can pay your bills and start taking your law practice seriously."

For the first time ever, he shot me a thoughtful glance. "You think so, Al? Well, how do I go about it?"

"I'll ask Carl Hurley [the ex-college professor with a national following as an after dinner comic]," I promised.

Hurley loved the idea, but his agent refused to help and told Hurley to stay away from Gatewood. "You are the clean funny man who gets all the gigs at family and church events," he reminded Carl. "Gatewood would roll 'em in the aisles on the campuses, but he doesn't belong on our team."

A week later, when I reported back, Gatewood took Carl Hurley's rejection with grace. "That's all right, Al," he said gently. "I've got a better plan."

"Willie Nelson called. He wants me to join him on his bus for six weeks on the road. After he does the shows, we'll smoke a little pot together."

# Part IX
## *Who They Were*

## Chapter 34

# A Baker's Dozen

*March 29, 1998*

The coal baron and entrepreneur John Caldwell Calhoun Mayo, who was the richest man in Kentucky at the beginning of the twentieth century, is remembered, if at all, for devising the iniquitous broad-form deed. By contrast, at the close of the century, another self-made Kentuckian of wealth and influence, W.T. Young of Lexington, has given millions to education and will be honored this week with the dedication of the William T. Young Library at the University of Kentucky.

Arguments over schools, crime, abortion, the environment and brick-and-mortar projects have their high road moments, but too many lawmakers remain mired in the ignorance and bigotry of our often sorry past.

With no map, legislators are trying to cope with challenges for the year 2000 without really understanding how we got where we are from where we were as a state one hundred years ago.

When the doors open in the Young library, let's draw a new "map," researching and writing about Kentuckians who have been influential during this century. Here are some who come to mind. Half are public citizen types; the others authors with impressive insights. There are more, perhaps equally significant, but for a short list here are my candidates:

# The Leaders

## *John C.C. Mayo (1864–1914)*

This mogul opened up Eastern Kentucky for coal and timber exploitation. His broad-form deed never envisioned strip mining. The royalties he paid and the jobs he created at the time were considered good money. Later, the devil was in strip mining abuses. It wasn't until 1988 that the broad-form deed's stranglehold on property rights was broken. To understand the special interests' influence on government in our time, begin with Mayo's, shall we say, crooked trail to Frankfort.

## *Judge Robert Worth Bingham (1871–1937)*

Lawyer, publisher, reform politician, he shaped the Louisville we know. The *Courier-Journal* he acquired became a progressive force in the state through two more generations of Binghams.

## *Madeline McDowell Breckinridge (1872–1920)*

Henry Clay's great-granddaughter was best known as a crusader for women's suffrage. A courageous campaigner for other social reforms, she influenced her husband's Lexington newspaper to support her causes. Born an aristocrat, she experienced tragedies and triumphs worthy of an Oscar-winning film.

## *Earle Chester Clements (1896–1985)*

With all respect to A.B. "Happy" Chandler, Clements was arguably the first "modern" governor (1947–50), one of the most innovative in history. As a U.S. senator, he forged an enduring bond with Lyndon B. Johnson. He also blazed a factional path for other progressive governors—Bert Combs, Lawrence Wetherby, Edward Breathitt, Wendell Ford and Julian Carroll, all of whom acknowledged him as a mentor. You have to know Clements's complicated career to appreciate his great enemies, including Chandler.

Governor Earle C. Clements (1947–50) resigned a year early to take a seat in the U.S. Senate. After losing the seat to Republican Thurston Morton in 1956, he managed the successful 1959 election campaign for governor of Bert T. Combs and returned to Washington as an influential lobbyist in 1960. He died at his home in Morganfield on March 12, 1995, at age eighty-eight. *Courtesy of Kentucky Historical Society.*

### *Muhammad Ali (1942– )*

Three times, he was the world heavyweight champion of boxing and so much more. Ali is the most widely known Kentuckian of this century and perhaps the strongest figure in American sports in this era. He endured scorn and exile from boxing for protesting the draft and the Vietnam War on religious grounds, as a converted Muslim. Ali survives as a national hero and a figure of hope, inspiration and principle to millions of people of color all over the world.

## The Authors

### *Thomas Merton (1915–1968)*

At a monastery near Bardstown, Merton wrote books and articles about contemplation and the spiritual life that found a worldwide audience. His respect for non-Christian faiths and cultural integrity and his compassion for those who suffered in the social upheavals of our time made him a figure of international influence.

### *Harry M. Caudill (1922–1990)*

Lawyer, historian, political moralist, he focused the world's attention on the plight of Appalachia. *Night Comes to the Cumberlands* is a seminal book, like Rachel Carson's *Silent Spring*, that sounded a righteous trumpet the country could not ignore.

### *Thomas D. Clark (1903–2005)*

Dr. Clark, the Mississippi-born historian, professor, civic activist and author was described by one college president as our most distinguished Kentuckian.

Thomas Merton, the famous monk and author at the Abbey of Gethsemani near Bardstown at whose grave, another monk told Al Smith, the Dalai Lama paid a visit, bowed reverently and then tied the yellow sash from his waist around the simple white cross that was its marker. *Courtesy of UK Special Collections.*

Besides his books, he was the champion who inspired a new state library and a new history center. Almost singlehandedly, he saved our past.

## *Robert Penn Warren (1905–1989)*

America's first poet laureate whose texts influenced the teaching of poetry and fiction everywhere. Two of his many novels—*All the King's Men* and *Night Rider*—speak vividly to the problem of power and political corruption, echoing lessons from the dark and bloody ground of his boyhood home in Western Kentucky.

## *Harriette Simpson Arnow (1908–1986)*

Her novel *The Dollmaker* is about a family of Eastern Kentuckians who move to Detroit in search of wartime factory jobs, a transformation so affecting that we really see a larger picture: the brutish uprooting of rural America. This is the big World War II book we complained we didn't have because we were looking for it from the battlefield, not the home front. And we didn't realize it would be written by a Kentucky woman.

Her experiences living in wartime Detroit, crowded with factory workers, after she grew up in rural southeast Kentucky inspired insights in the fiction by novelist Harriette Arnow. Interviewed by Al Smith for KET, she suggested that Gertie Nevels, the wood carving artist hero of *The Dollmaker*, learned through her tragedies in Detroit "to live without myths." *Courtesy of UK Special Collections.*

Add three more prominent Kentuckians and you have a baker's dozen for study—Alben Barkley, the U.S. senator who became a beloved vice-president; Martha Layne Collins, our first female governor; and Wendell Berry, the man of letters and advocate for the family farm.

Barkley's story is the New Deal's impact on Kentucky. As Franklin D. Roosevelt's majority leader, Barkley was there when Kentuckians turned to Washington to help them do what they couldn't do for themselves. The Western Kentucky lakes, TVA, farm assistance, Fort Knox, Fort Campbell, Social Security, protection for unions—Barkley was involved. When you study him, you learn about his friendly rival and one of the greatest Republican Kentuckians since Lincoln, John Sherman Cooper.

Collins was underrated, but her stock is rising as we comprehend the impact of her economic development efforts. As the Young library doors open, the stronger aspects of our economy include seventy-six thousand jobs in 350 auto-related plants. The auto industry accounts for 22 percent of our gross state income. The investment for Toyota and 125 plants developed after Collins signed the Georgetown deal account for $3 billion and twenty-five thousand of those auto jobs, a third of the total.

Back on the farm, Wendell Berry worries about *The Unsettling of America: Culture and Agriculture*, the title of one of his acclaimed books on what is happening to our land and rural people.

Berry is a traditionalist whose expressive voice on behalf of the environment and the individual is a call to our conscience from the distractions of materialism.

So that's thirteen to read about at the new William T. Young Library, electronically accessible across the commonwealth to any thoughtful citizen who might replace or add to this list with equally defensible names. When they turn on the computers and uncrate the files, learning more about Kentucky should be an important priority. The study of Kentucky is the map to our future and can take place in a library that some of us think is grander and greater than a basketball arena, a spectacular gift from the old century to the new.

# Part X

# *In Our Time (Appreciations)*

## *Chapter 35*

# The Last Rhea in Logan County

*April 13, 2008*

Lillian Clark Rhea Noe, the retired Logan County librarian who died last month in Russellville, Kentucky, at ninety-one, was one the few survivors of a long ago campaign for governor between her father and the colorful Albert B. "Happy" Chandler. It was a race that Chandler won, splitting the state Democratic Party into two factions for the next forty years. Despite the acrimony, the race launched an era of generally progressive governors who historians say were stronger and more effective than Governor Steve Beshear, or either of his predecessors in the last eight years.

Widow of a circuit judge and mother of the current Logan County attorney, Thomas A. Noe III, she was the last of four children who grew up in the same house with a politically powerful Thomas S. Rhea, and two uncles—John, a former congressman and judge, and Albert, an editor. The three Rheas also owned a weekly newspaper and two banks, while leading a courthouse machine that had controlled most local elections in Logan County since before the Civil War.

Lillian Noe befriended me when I came to Kentucky fifty years ago to edit the *News-Democrat*, which her family had lost, along with the banks and the governorship, in the Great Depression. We grew even closer as her husband, the judge, Tom Noe Jr., and I shared a struggle with alcoholism. In 1968, when I was sober, she was among the local investors who helped me buy the paper, a business in which the family first was involved in 1807.

A woman of intellectual and spiritual depth, she never ran for office, but she managed the library for twenty-three years with a populist concern for making it accessible, doubling its size, expanding its branches and encouraging the poorest of kids and their parents to find inspiration and hope in books. Enduring a succession of tragedies—the loss of two sons, a son-in-law and her husband's early death—she disdained the rantings of the religious right, but her own profound faith was the central message at her funeral in Russellville.

Lillian was nineteen in 1935 when Tom Rhea, a friend of President Franklin Roosevelt and heir apparent to Governor Ruby Laffoon, was challenged by Happy Chandler. Rhea was sixty-eight, the state highway chief and party leader in Western Kentucky. As he and Laffoon left the state on a Washington-bound train to see Roosevelt about patronage issues, Chandler, only thirty-six but already lieutenant governor, called a special session of the legislature to revise archaic election rules that would have favored Rhea.

Perhaps only A.B. (Ben) Chandler Jr., still publisher of the Chandler family newspaper, the *Woodford Sun* at Versailles, retains the same vivid memories that Lillian Noe had of how his father duped her father into accepting a change of the Democratic primary from a convention, which assuredly would have chosen Rhea, to a primary plus a runoff that Chandler eventually won, the only second primary Kentucky has held.

After a bitter Rhea supported Chandler's Republican opponent to no avail in the fall, it became the precedent Chandler cited whenever he bolted to Republicans in four decades of conflict with other Democrats. Although Rhea's legacy, beginning with Earle Clements, was the more liberal wing of governors, his own career was finished. Chandler went on to become a U.S. Senator and national commissioner of baseball and won a second term as governor. Happy's grandson, U.S. Representative Ben Chandler, and Tom Rhea's grandson Tom Noe, the Logan County attorney, are chips off the giant oaks: easy to meet, likeable, decent, well-read, with a passion for history but scant enthusiasm for what it takes to claw to the top in today's politics. When Ben Chandler didn't run for governor last year, one of his friends wasn't surprised: "Why should he leave Washington, where he connects with the world, to come back home and face four years of telling some guy from Greasy Creek with no teeth why he can't have a road?"

In Logan County, where they now vote Republican and admire Mitch McConnell, everybody knows that the younger Tom Noe is a liberal Democrat like his mother. But he is smart, helpful and, like her, kind.

Like Ben Chandler, he is respected and very electable at his present pay grade.

The world of personal politics in which their grandfathers flourished has vanished. The governorship is won by raising obscene amounts of cash paid to image-makers, pollsters and consultants who tell the candidates what to say and ill prepare them for victory. Nobody seems to care about history, and that may be a problem for the Chandler and Rhea grandsons. They do.

## *Chapter 36*

# Lucille Little and Friends

*May 7, 2000*

In the first spring of a new century, a gift to Centre College by a wealthy Lexington woman with deep roots in Kentucky celebrates good works in the last century by a husband and wife who came here as strangers from Boston nearly fifty years ago and never went back.

A $1 million endowed lecture series, named for O. Leonard and Lillian Henken Press and initiated by a $500,000 challenge grant from their friend Lucille Caudill Little, honors what Mrs. Little calls "the creativity they inspired in others" in their long careers as state employees. Len Press was the founding director of Kentucky Educational Television in 1963. Lillian Press was the founding director who opened the Governor's Scholars Program at Centre College in 1983.

Arriving in 1952, they planned to stay only a year—he teaching broadcast courses at University of Kentucky and she writing ad copy for a radio station. Not all the doors immediately opened for a young couple from the north, but they soon made many friends anyway; their careers took off with challenges in educational TV and social services, and they forgot about leaving.

As he became a force in national public broadcasting and she a top administrator in mental health programs in the 1970s, the Presses put down their own roots in Kentucky. To promote KET, "I would go anywhere I could find three people," says Len Press. "That's how we met so many Kentuckians," his wife adds.

Their success in selling innovative educational and social enterprises to a succession of governors and community leaders disputes claims that Kentuckians won't accept newcomers who are change agents. Their story should hearten talented outsiders who are considering a move to Kentucky.

We go back together. When Len started KET's *Comment on Kentucky* in 1974 he risked me as host. Later, Lil worked for me at the Appalachian Regional Commission in Washington before starting the Governor's Scholars Program. But my bias is that of a witness to their positive influence on public policies. And that is the purpose of the Press lecture series.

Although the endowment and the first speaker, presidential historian Arthur Schlesinger, were announced at Centre in Danville last month, Mrs. Little, ninety-one, continued to celebrate by hosting the Presses and others recently at the Keeneland races.

With a reserved table in the clubhouse and a preferred box outside, legacies from W. Paul Little, who made millions in horses, real estate and tobacco, his widow is a killer handicapper. Pausing to collect on a fistful of two-dollar bets, she reflects on her guests. "I don't know many people like Len and Lil who have designed institutions that will survive them, that encourage creativity the way KET and the Governor's Scholars do."

In marrying Paul Little in 1937, Lucille Caudill, daughter of a prominent Eastern Kentucky family, gave up dreams of being a singer, actress and dancer in New York, but Little backed his wife's leadership in the arts in the Bluegrass State. Before dying in 1990, he blessed a plan to give most of their fortune to the arts and education, with emphasis on creativity. They were childless, but in the search to enrich other people's children, Lucille Little met the Presses.

KET, to which Mrs. Little gave $1 million, now reaches nearly a million viewers in the commonwealth with classical music, dance, drama and other shows. It is the largest state network in the PBS system. The Governor's Scholar's program, established in 1983, will soon add a third campus. It has received some $400,000 in Little money. Over eleven thousand Kentucky high school students have taken part since Lil Press opened the first summer with visits from astronauts, opera singers and a Nobel laureate scientist.

Finally retirees, the Presses scan a racing form with Mrs. Little as she mentions donating to another interest, the terra cotta horses from China in an art exhibit that opened last week at the Kentucky Horse Park.

Green eyes and red hair, matched by a stylish suit and blouse in her trademark vivid colors, anything but somber, Lucille Little is laughing. It's the voice of a very deaf elderly lady, once a spirited girl from Rowan

Lucille Little (second from right) was honored, with her friends Len and Lillian Press at a party at Centre College hosted by President John Roush (right). The event inaugurated an annual speakers' program, the Press Lecture, which was endowed by Mrs. Little. *Photo by Martha Helen Smith.*

County in singing classes at Manhattan's Julliard. Now a beloved queen of the Bluegrass, she strains to hear what horse her friends bet on. The answer comes with a chuckle in a Boston accent. They are a trio: different feathers, different notes, different birds, but warbling together—happy in the beautiful Kentucky springtime.

When Mrs. Little died at ninety-three on October 8, 2002, in Lexington, the Little Foundation was ranked ninth in Kentucky by total dollars donated. Now managed by the Bluegrass Community Foundation, gifts are awarded quarterly to develop creativity, mainly through the creative arts.

The Governor's Scholars Program, operating on three host college sites, has grown from the first class of 230 students in 1983 to 1,000 in 2012.

*Chapter 37*

# Public Servant, First Class

*December 3, 2008*

Much of Kentucky history is remembered in the names of its elected or cultural heroes—a Henry Clay or Happy Chandler, a Loretta Lynn or Colonel Sanders—and certainly the athletes, such as Dan Issel, Muhammad Ali. Even a horse: Secretariat and Man o' War come to mind.

But those of us who labor in journalism, which is sometimes called the first draft of history, know that we can't do our job without "sources." These are the folks behind the scenes who make government run, or manage a campaign for election, or switch on the stage lights for great performances. It is they who are also willing to teach us what is really happening as the words are written or after the lights have dimmed and the stars are moving to the next public encounter.

Such a "source," but also a change agent for good government, was Robert D. "Bob" Bell, who died at eighty-three this week in Lexington, the town where he was born when it was a community of horse people and tobacco farmers about the size of Covington.

His father was a shoe salesman and his mother managed a school cafeteria. Without the GI Bill benefits after his service in World War II, Bob doubted he would have gone to UK. But his government-assisted college education meant so much to him that he was forever after passionate about helping other Kentuckians go to school.

Bob channeled his idealism into a career of government and corporate service for leaders who used his administrative skills to do really good things—first working in high posts for five governors in Frankfort where he helped build and manage parks and highways, protect natural resources, boost education funding and wisely allocate revenues.

Under one governor, Julian Carroll, who deserves more credit than he has gotten for some of his successes, the attacks on Bell from the coal industry when Bell was secretary of natural resources were so unrelenting and Carroll's support for Bell was so wavering that Bell resigned. He had no job, but it was an act of principle. In the mid 1970s that was the prelude for a memorable decade as an executive at Ashland Oil Company where he encouraged his bosses to focus their advertising, charities and public relations on better education—a process which helped all Kentuckians and raised the image of Ashland as a good corporate citizen.

The paid obituary notices and brief news stories detailed some of the specifics of Bell's career—governors he served, organizations he helped create (Advocates for Higher Education, Governor's Scholars, Prichard Committee), but there was no space for the stories of old-timers at the funeral Wednesday. They remembered Bell's wit and his corrosive complaints against the shortcomings of politicians with whom he worked, but also his generous willingness to forgive them for a weekend of companionable fishing trips.

Not much of a fisherman, I offer a note about books and Bell. In the late 1980s, he volunteered to help the struggling Thomas D. Clark Endowment Fund, created to support the University Press of Kentucky which Clark, the noted historian, had founded many years earlier. Working several days a week from a desk in the Press office, and often driving Dr. Clark on "tin cup" missions to see wealthy friends across the commonwealth, Bell and another volunteer, Ted Broida of Lexington, raised nearly $1.5 million. These efforts underwrote the successful publications of two invaluable projects, *The Encyclopedia of Kentucky* in 1992 and the *Encyclopedia of Louisville* in 2001.

Inspired by Bell's commitment, a new generation of Clark Foundation trustees is seeking funding for two more encyclopedias, one for Northern Kentucky and one on African American life in the commonwealth.

Never seeking the spotlight, his was a career that mixed political conviction—he was a New Dealer kind of Democrat—and non-biased administration: a role model to be remembered, in these troubled times

## Chapter 38

# A Brilliant Professor

*January 2005*

My youngest grandchild, Ava Russell Major, then ten weeks old, laughed for the first time last month. Her mother called from Connecticut to describe it as "a hearty laugh"—louder than the burping and pooping at Christmas.

Ava's Kentucky-born parents, Bill, from Louisville, and Ginny, from Lexington, now live near Hartford and the historic home owned by Mark Twain, the pen name of Samuel Clemens, when he was a rich and famous author. Twain, whose mother was born in Adair County, Kentucky, made millions of Americans laugh with his stories and lectures. But he also had a dark, gloomy side.

Guy Davenport, the multi-talented professor and author who died at seventy-seven last month, taught his literature students at University of Kentucky like Ava's father, who was inspired to become an English professor himself, to understand a paradox in Twain's work: that Twain was both comical and deeply pessimistic. Davenport taught his students why Ernest Hemingway said modern American literature started from one book by Mark Twain called *Huckleberry Finn.*

Davenport, one of the great teachers in UK's history, published several dozen books, among them a novel, collections of short stories, essays and works on art and of his own drawings. A Rhodes Scholar, his academic degrees were from Duke, Oxford and Harvard. In 1990, when he received a so-called genius award, a MacArthur Foundation grant for $365,000, he retired.

With its dire headlines of war and tsunamis, January was a hard month to get through. But in Connecticut, my Kentucky family had a new laughing child to love and the memory of a brilliant teacher to steady their faith in life's possibilities.

## *Chapter 39*

# A Prince of Western Kentucky

*August 30, 2006*

To the strains of classical music that he loved, friends gathered at the First Christian Church of Owensboro this week to mourn the death of attorney Morton J. Holbrook Jr., ninety-one, a prince of the region and a counselor to its power structure for over half a century. A graduate of Harvard law school, he never sought elective office, but for three decades he was at the elbow of Owensboro politicians, all Democrats, as they muscled their way to statewide dominance against challenges at the ballot box and in the courts.

Holbrook figured importantly in the rise and decline of a regional political base in which the principal players were Wendell Ford, who became a governor and U.S. senator; J.R. Miller, the hard-charging and wily utility executive who managed Ford's ascent; and Don Blandford, who emerged from a humble job as union butcher to win a seat in the state House. As speaker, he led enactment of the nationally acclaimed 1990 Kentucky Education Reform Act.

Short of stature, Holbrook compensated by becoming a skilled boxer in his youth, winning a couple of fist fights along the way, rising to the rank of major in World War II combat and staying fit all of his life with a dedication to sports no less intense than to music and literature. Unfailingly courteous in court, he kept his legal aides hustling under the rule that "if God could create Heaven and earth in seven days, this brief can be done in ten."

Attorney Morton Holbrook (left) and Historian Thomas D. Clark were among the commonwealth's leading elders when they met for a roundtable chaired at Shaker Village at Pleasant Hill by Al Smith.

Holbrook and Wilson Wyatt of Louisville headed the campaign that amended the state constitution in 1975 to modernize the courts and require all judges to be lawyers. (It was an upset victory. "Morton, why didn't you and Wilson tell us you were going to win?" complained one county judge. "And then we'd a beat the damn thing!")

As chair of the Council on Higher Education in the 1980s, Holbrook promoted with Blandford and Governor Martha Layne Collins a community college for Owensboro that many in Davies County would prize as their greatest service. But in a new era in which our grassroots politics have been replaced by media consultants and many counties have lost cohesive leadership, it is instructive to understand that Holbrook's early crusades for reform owed much to the nitty-gritty of backroom deals that crossed county lines, one handshake at a time. In his late years, he bridged the "old politics" of Ford and Miller and the media era ushered in by the glitzy election of Governor John Y. Brown Jr. in 1979.

Described by his minister as a multi-talented "treasure" and by other attorneys as one who could have excelled anywhere, I thought he was the most gifted man I ever knew in Kentucky. The son of a rural banker, he returned to Owensboro after graduating from University of Kentucky and Harvard Law School. At Harvard, he was a classmate in the mid-1930s of two other brilliant Kentuckians, Edward F. Prichard Jr. and Philip Ardery, who also came home to careers in which all three men promoted political causes that reflected the idealism of Franklin D. Roosevelt's New Deal. Prichard is dead but left a legacy of emphasis on education, which was also championed by Holbrook. Ardery was an influential advocate for rural electrification, the cause that brought J.R. Miller to Owensboro in the 1960s to manage the Green River Rural Electric Cooperative.

With Holbrook as his lawyer, Miller developed the Big Rivers Electric Corp., a huge generator of coal-fired electricity to serve their vision of transforming the Green River country into an industrial complex on the scale of the Ruhr River Valley in Germany. Financed by low-cost loans from a federal program to electrify farms, Big Rivers did attract aluminum plants and other industries, and along the way, Miller created a network of political support that propelled Wendell Ford into the governorship in 1971 and elected his ally Walter D. Huddleston to the U.S. Senate in 1972.

By the time Ford was elected to the Senate and Julian Carroll, another western Kentucky politician who benefited from Miller, became governor in 1974, Big Rivers was overloaded with debt—a challenge that kept Miller and Holbrook scrambling for political bailouts for the next twenty years. Holbrook defended Ford and Miller from prosecution over claims that they had concealed campaign contributions. Ford and Carroll were unscathed by grand jury probes of their patronage dealings, but Blandford was not so lucky. His public career ended in 1992 when, despite a defense by Holbrook and his son Allen, he was convicted of taking a bribe. Before its reorganization, Big Rivers was tarnished by a bribery scandal, and Holbrook was criticized for failing to uncover it internally.

The Ford-Miller-Blandford combine ran out of gas a decade ago, but leaving the steps of the church on J.R. Miller Boulevard, after the Holbrook funeral, a visitor could see the fruits of their labors—a $20 million Riverfront Park Center for which Holbrook was a mover and shaker, new buildings at the community college where five thousand students are enrolled, a Morton Holbrook Judicial Center, an art museum that is the envy of larger cities and a $3 million bicycle path in a green belt around the city. Across the Ohio River, a new $300 million William Natcher Bridge is a breathtaking monument to political perseverance and a Ford- Miller-Holbrook ally. In an Owensboro bank is $40 million for more improvements secured, ironically, by Wendell Ford's final nemesis, Republican Senator Mitch McConnell.

In Frankfort, former Owensboro mayor David Adkisson, who was a sparkplug for many of these improvements, says that he has not forgotten some of the lessons he learned from the Democrats in the Owensboro of his youth. Now president of the Kentucky Chamber of Commerce, he is coordinating a big blowout in Washington this fall by the state's civic and business leadership—an appreciation dinner, to honor McConnell.

## *Chapter 40*

# The Advocate

*September 2010*

There will be a memorial service in Lexington Saturday for Robert F. Sexton, the advocate for better schools who died August 26 after an eighteen-month battle with esophageal cancer. He was sixty-eight. Described as a "celebration" of his life, the program will begin at 1:30 p.m. at the Mitchell Fine Arts Center at Transylvania University. The public is invited.

One of our great social reformers and a political liberal and progressive when many Kentuckians disliked those who seemed such, Bob was an even tempered idealist, a college history professor in his early career who turned public policy advocate and engaged the outside world with plain language intended to persuade rather than offend.

I admired him immensely. The best words to be spoken at this memorial will call for more citizens to follow his example and, as he urged graduates in a commencement address this spring, to become involved in solving problems—from the grassroots to the state capitol.

As the voice of the Prichard Committee for Academic Excellence, Bob was a champion for three decades of the movement that was instrumental in securing passage of the Kentucky Education Reform Act (KERA) in 1990. The one-hundred-member committee was named for its first chairman, Edward F. Prichard Jr., a political figure whose disgrace in a voting scandal in his youth was overcome in late life by his visionary crusade for schools.

Six years after Prichard's death, Sexton helped the legislature craft KERA, perhaps the most sweeping educational reform in the United States. Then, as the Prichard Committee's first and only executive director, he battled for the next twenty years to keep the cause alive—first by recruiting leaders and funding for the committee, then by defending KERA from its critics and urging lawmakers to add improvements, such as pre-kindergarten, a program still languishing for lack of tax support.

Indifference or outright hostility to academic progress has always been an issue in Kentucky. Historian and Prichard Committee stalwart Thomas Clark wrote that "whatever pioneering immigrants lugged across the Appalachians in the late 18th century, they seem not to have brought along a burning zeal to educate their children." But Sexton took the long view. "If you are doing this work [for better education] you want to be an optimist," he told a reporter. As the commencement speaker for Bellarmine University only a few months before his death, Bob proudly noted significant gains from KERA that have moved Kentucky from the bottom to almost the middle rank of U.S. schools.

Nevertheless, "average" must not be the goal for Kentucky kids "when prosperity today depends on education and the brain power it creates," he said. Improving schools is a challenge for elected leaders, not just for figures of great wealth like Oprah Winfrey or Bill Gates. The need, he said, is for "all other people who roll up their sleeves and decide on their own to help their churches or their schools or their clubs solve problems. "

To improve the schools, Bob was a "social entrepreneur," as his wife, Pam, described him, engaged in a civic life so extensive that a listing fills three pages ranging from small town Rotary Club talks to lectures at Harvard. The national boards he served on suggest how far from Kentucky he ranged to share his experience and find grants for his committee.

From his sickbed in the last months of his life, he wrote newspaper columns on the need for pre-school investments and warned that the latest spare budget was "another step backward for Kentucky's kids." On an afternoon in late August, he asked his assistant to notify the papers that he had a comment on Kentucky's loss of millions in the federally funded "race to the top." But before the reporters could call back next day, Kentucky had also lost him.

Who would doubt that Bob Sexton, the young Louisville high school football captain and class president who went to Yale, could have been a success in business, the professions or politics? But he never ran for elective office. He didn't invent a new machine, create a financial empire or head a giant corporation. Instead, he tackled our most important challenge: how to help our children become competitive in a knowledge economy. He never claimed that the end was in sight, but who denies that he made a positive, inspiring difference?

*Chapter 41*

# Hero of the Mountains

*February 23, 2012*

Michael Lee Mullins, the executive director of the Hindman Settlement School, died last Sunday when the heart he had given in three decades of service to the people of his native mountains, finally wore out as he exercised in a gym. He was sixty-three. When I met him, he was thirty years old and capturing my attention for his advocacy of education, the arts and a better life at the grassroots of the region.

The son of a coal miner and the first of his family to graduate from college (earning two degrees), Mike had found his mission in rescuing the historic settlement school from death by broken pipes and decayed buildings when he took charge in the winter of 1977. He created a new role for the school, founded in 1902 when Knott County had no public system, sending art and music teachers into the hollows and, later, establishing a food bank and bookmobile routes. In a community of much poverty, "make do" or do without, he gave the people a higher vision by sponsoring performances of ballet companies, folk singers and classical guitarists. Eventually he started a writers' workshop, featuring the presence of poet and storyteller James Still, and helped begin a tutorial program for dyslexic kids.

Where there was much exploitation, Mike did nothing but good. He was a hero of Appalachia.

Mike Mullins spent a year of his childhood recovering from illness. He told the author of this book that his adult life of service at the Hindman Settlement School was committed to "giving back" to others in the spirit of what was given to him. *Photo by Roger Alford. Courtesy of the* Courier-Journal.

## *Chapter 42*

# Lady of Grace and Grit

*March 20, 2012*

While Lois Gray, who will be buried Friday at her beloved hometown of Glasgow, is credited with leading her family in transforming the little building company she and her husband founded there into an international construction powerhouse now based in Lexington, her legacy is much more than that of a lady in a hard hat.

A woman of exceptional grace and beauty, elegant manners, slender figure and stylish dress, she looked a little incongruous under that work site helmet in the company publicity pictures. But her lovely smile; her soft speech of welcome to clients from all over the world who attended her Derby parties, then returned to sign a contract; and her steely determination to help her children make good on every promise became the public face of the brand her four sons and their two sisters called "The Gray Way" of doing business.

She carried the title of chairman for nearly fifty years while the sons took turns as CEO, with one, Jim, becoming mayor of Lexington. They and their employees executed the operating plans that made them one of the nation's most admired design/build construction firms.

They were building strip shopping centers, schools and small-town nursing homes and I was a weekly newspaper editor when I met the Grays forty years ago in western Kentucky, mistaking Howard, the twenty-three-year-old president, for the office boy. Newly widowed at fifty-one, her youngest

The mother who helped her children weather the ups and downs of a family start-up business after losing her husband when he was young, Lois Gray was admired for civic and business leadership. The company was flourishing when she died at ninety-one in 2012. *Courtesy of Gray family.*

son only seven, Lois had little time to grieve when her husband, James Norris Gray, a popular civic booster in Glasgow, died suddenly of cancer. An artist at heart but raised a princess in rural Barren County, the daughter of a renowned country doctor and a schoolteacher, she ignored advice to shut down, charmed mentors into helping and inspired her young sons into picking up their Dad's dreams.

I knew them when they were insolvent, mired in debt but saved in part by their mother's gritty resolve to not let them fail. Despite her deep roots in Glasgow, she blessed their decision to broaden their horizon and relocate the company in Lexington where they won the largest sub-contract of any Kentucky firm chosen to build the Toyota plant at Georgetown.

That was a big step in the direction they have moved to achieve a significant niche as a builder of choice for foreign countries—over 350 Japanese companies to date and some 400 in total for companies also from Korea, Australia, Austria and China.

Early on, customers and friends understood that Lois believed a lot of life was about service. In World War II, as a WAVE officer, she lived under marine guard in Washington, where she plotted positions of the wartime fleet at naval headquarters. Never forgetting that personal history, eventually she took her large brood of grandchildren to Normandy to visit the memorials to the D-Day invasion. Learning from her father, a leader in Kentucky health crusades, that all of us should be concerned for the needs of our fellow citizens, Lois and her sons served on college and university boards across the commonwealth, raised money for the arts and education and helped build the Thomas Clark History Center in Frankfort.

Lured by the beauty of the Maine coast, freed from business cares as her company stabilized, she spent happy summer months in her last years painting watercolors around Camden, Maine. Then the memory thief of Alzheimer's called to claim her. But while there was pulse in her veins on the last day of her life Monday at her Lexington home, the gathered family, realizing what she would want to hear from the world she was leaving, began to sing at her bedside. Remembering happy times on Derby Day, they sang, "My Old Kentucky Home."

# Part XI
## *Swept Away*

## *Chapter 43*

# A Prayer for New Orleans

*August 30, 2005*

Confronting the most heartbreaking natural disaster in Gulf Coast history, the newspaper where I once worked in New Orleans, the *Times-Picayune*, its offices and presses flooding, put out one edition early this week—an electronic version under the stark headline, "CATASTROPHIC." Then staff members headed for Houma, a bayou city 60 miles to the west.

As the *Times-Picayune* editors scramble to publish in print again on borrowed presses on high ground, the tensions and challenges might resemble those in the 1937 Ohio River flood in Louisville when the *Courier-Journal* reported rescues from Louisville streets under water.

This week, as the disaster pictures on TV grew more and more grim, my thoughts repeatedly turned to a hurricane that struck New Orleans when I was there in the 1950s, the worst weather story I have ever covered. On that assignment, I worked twenty-four hours straight, and then another week without a break, but horrific as it was—several hundred dead on the Louisiana Gulf Coast and a strong hit on New Orleans itself—we got the paper out, on time and on our own presses. It was not the calamity that has now befallen the city that I called home for ten years of my life, 1947–1957. We did not wonder if the soul of the town had died.

This time, the death toll still rising, the devastation so widespread, the survivors so stunned and uprooted, the cost of Hurricane Katrina is being reckoned in many ways, yet it is unthinkable that New Orleans will not be

A child is among many saved by rescue workers, but 1,800 lives were lost in the week of Katrina. *Photo by Vincent Laforet, courtesy of Vincent Laforet/*The New York Times*/Redux.*

rebuilt. But, as never before, after the wars, storms, floods and fevers that have afflicted New Orleans, many Americans may fear that her distinctive spirit has drowned in the roiled muddy waters—that, indeed, like some evil voodoo queen of prophecy sent from hell to steal the psyche of the city, Katrina *was* "the big one" long awaited by a unique place on borrowed time.

While the old city may emerge from the floodwaters decked out in billions of dollars of new timber, steel and mortar, it could become just a theme park, *New York Times* reporter Peter Applebome speculated—"the glitter of Bourbon Street without the grit that surrounds it."

It was in "old" New Orleans, the Original Old Absinthe House Bar, in the French Quarter on Bourbon Street, where I first paused to get my bearings in November 1947 after I told the dean at Vanderbilt University I was dropping out to become a writer down there. Having already expelled me once for failure to attend classes, the dean seemed bemused. "Do they know you are coming?" he asked. No one in my family knew, but the first night after I got off the bus from Nashville, I began investing half the one hundred dollars I brought with me in a new friend. He was Owen Brennan, an ambitious Irishman who owned the Absinthe House and told me he planned to open a restaurant across the street.

So began the story of my life in New Orleans, somewhat expurgated, that I told my grandsons, Connor, fifteen, and Evan, twelve, on a visit there last Memorial Day with Martha Helen, their grandmother. We were staying at the Monteleone, William Faulkner's favorite hotel, where Liberace and Rosemary Clooney performed when they were as young as I, and where, on Royal Street across from the hotel, I once spied Ernest Hemingway in safari shirt and khaki shorts peering at some jewelry in the window of an antique shop.

The streetcar named Desire ran on Royal in those days, I told my grandsons, but I skipped the night Cammy Carroll (a former debutante, but that's not quite her name) stormed out of Lafitte's Blacksmith Shop (a bar) swearing to me that "that faggot is trying to put the make on my husband!" Her handsome young husband was a descendant of an early Louisiana governor; our accused drinking companion was the playwright Tennessee Williams. Was not this better than college, or what?

When I came to Kentucky, ten years later, I had finished up all my friends in New Orleans. My future in the Big Easy was over. But in Kentucky, where we make the whiskey that almost killed me in Louisiana, I learned another lesson. With the help of other recovering alcoholics, I learned how not to drink.

It was fourteen years before I returned to New Orleans, but, sober, I searched out the closest of my former friends. Still living in the grace of a magical city that we used to say "care forgot," they had forgotten to care that I had disappointed them. They welcomed me back.

There isn't much bad that hasn't happened in New Orleans, including the looting by frightened, suffering and desperate people this week, the organized graft I covered on the police beat and my own misdeeds fifty years ago. But a community that has also shared so much joy and forgiven so many sinners deserves to live and be redeemed. That's what I thought when I heard the Louisiana governor ask for prayers. So I pray for that.

Four months later, in early January 2006, when three of my friends and I arrived in the French Quarter from Kentucky, we had made the trip in a long day, thanks to the stamina of the young driver with two famous Kentucky names, Clay Barkley. Outside K-Paul's Kitchen, where the wait-line used to extend along the sidewalk, Paul Prudhomme, the famous chef-proprietor, was seated in a wheelchair and waving a big white napkin to lead a little pickup band in riffs from "When The Saints Go Marching In." On the nearly deserted street, he was hustling late-night dinner customers. Inside, we had no difficulty securing a table. A waiter said his boss had brought the staff back to reopen the restaurant by offering housing in rented trailers. Most of the few other diners were relief workers, served by waiters who, like ours, seemed eager to relate colorful, often shocking, memories of their Katrina experiences.

Next day, one of our group, Mark Neikirk, managing editor of the *Cincinnati Post* and *Kentucky Post* that have since folded, called a friend, the local AP bureau chief, to guide us through the wreckage we had come to see. The depressing tour was brightened somewhat with hopeful commentary by our Kentucky experts, Sam Thomas, the author of books on historic Louisville, and Barkley, who had earned degrees in urban planning before he became a lawyer. I did what I could as a raconteur of stories from my decade on the New Orleans papers, including the 1948 campaign visit by Clay's great-great-grandfather, Alben Barkley of Paducah, who always brought hope.

Now, seven years on, aided by billions in federal reconstruction dollars, there were signs of recovery: the population of New Orleans was reported to have grown faster than any other major U.S. city in the fifteen months after the 2010 census. A surprising number of folks who fled after hurricanes Katrina and Rita came home. From a pre-storm tally of 452,000, population fell to 223,000 but had increased to 361,000. Nearly nine million tourists spent $5.5 billion in 2011.

On the negative side, New Orleans sought federal help to fight a high crime rate and inefficiencies and corruption in the police department, as of my days on the beat. My old paper, the *Times-Picayune*, which had won praise for its Pulitzer Prize–winning coverage of the storms and after, lost half its newsroom in layoffs by the Newhouse owners who cut it to three days a week and planned to convert to a primarily digital news product. New Orleans will be the largest city in the country without a daily newspaper.

The good news about New Orleans obscured crisis facts about Louisiana's coastal erosion of twenty-five to thirty-six square miles a year. This is a "working coast," environmentalists stress, supporting a critical infrastructure vital to the national economy. Without coastal restoration, there will be severe consequences. But like Kentucky, with its long history of tolerating abuses by the coal industry, Louisiana has been frighteningly careless of its natural resources. More than prayer is needed, and for much more than New Orleans.

# *Chapter 44*

# Remembering Flight 5191

*Delivered at Lexington Community Memorial Service for victims and families, September 10, 2006*

## In Memoriam

Living near the Lexington airport, I heard the sirens early that Sunday morning, August 27, but I went back to sleep until the phone rang, not knowing they were first responders to an airplane crash. The voice on the phone was my son in Louisville, telling me to turn on the television.

For the rest of the day, I watched, listened and talked on the phone as the tragic news united Lexington into a community of shock, concern and grief.

The failure of a liftoff by Flight 5191 and the deaths of forty-nine aboard had suddenly brought us all to ground, focused on a tiny wooded blur concealing most of the wreckage of lost hopes and lives at the edge of the TV screens.

Before and behind the cameras, the journalists, many of them my colleagues and friends, scrambled to get the news, all bad. On the radio, another of my friends, who had lost his own wife in an accident a month before, was on the air ten hours to anchor a national broadcast of the story—"from coast to coast," as we used to say.

In the Reflection Garden at the Arboretum at Lexington, a memorial to victims of air disaster depicts birds in flight. *Photo by Martha Helen Smith.*

And as we used to gather around disaster in the little western Kentucky town of Russellville where I was the editor nearly fifty years ago, so did the citizens of Kentucky's second-largest city become like a small town where everybody knew somebody who was in deep trouble over Flight 5191.

As the ambulances pulled out of the field where the Comair went down, and a lone survivor was rushed by police car to the Chandler Medical Center at UK, I remembered the operating room in the county hospital at Russellville those many years ago where the only two surgeons frantically labored to save the lives of three strangers in a car crash that had killed two other persons who were unknown to any of us.

Normally, those surgeons hated each other—they were jealous competitors—but this was all forgotten in the rush to repair the broken bodies of fellow human beings in grave peril. At the side of these surgeons, in gowns and masks, assisting as best they could, were the other doctors in that rural county, maybe five, and not all of them pals, either.

We were one community that night, and a half century later, it was the same way in Lexington on August 27, 2006, and for days after when we shared hugs and flowers, hot meals, music and tears, and citizens would hold up those signs for passing buses of relatives: "We are praying for you."

One of the reporters who talked to several family members of victims said he was amazed by their strength and perspective. They wanted to describe their final memories, the last talk, the last smile, even, in one case, the last dance. It was simultaneously heart-wrenching and heartwarming to do these interviews, he said, and to get such personal glimpses into their families, their achievements and their lives. As a result, the whole community got to know these forty-nine people and why they were so special to those who loved them.

"I found myself privately mourning for folks I had never heard of just days ago," the reporter told me.

## The Road of Gratitude

Why does a God of love allow such a tragedy to happen? Of course, this is a question theologians have pondered for years. As another reporter who covered this accident, a man of faith, wrote me, "We live in a world where children get leukemia, where terrorists knock down our tallest buildings, where planes crash." We are not exempt from suffering, but, like Job of the Bible, we might learn that by trust in God we can become eternally secure, the reporter suggested.

And yet, as a former governor of Kentucky, who lost a relative in an air disaster, said to me this week, don't tell people not to grieve. It's OK to rage, to let our sorrow get out. At the same time, he said, we have got to be comforted when so many people in this community grieve right along with us.

One of my children offers us some consoling lessons from a great Kentucky-born preacher, John Claypool, who lost a ten-year-old daughter to cancer when they lived in Louisville. Claypool said it is crazy to talk about our losses as "God's will." We don't know any such thing. We are finite, and we just don't understand everything about God. On the other hand, it is a dead-end to decide the universe is absurd because a child suffers and dies, Claypool said. This ignores countless other experiences of love and purpose and meaning in which we or they do not die. A third way, says Claypool, is "the road of gratitude"—to realize that life is a gift, and instead of staying mad because it was taken away, we should become grateful that we ever had it at all.

In the context of memory, catastrophe and recovery, we made safety improvements after the Beverly Hills nightclub fire; we strengthened our school buses and our drunk-driving laws after the Carrolton bus crash. Our tragedy at the airport, a horrible accident, is contemporary with our struggle to resolve the terrible issues of 9/11, which was an armed attack, and of Hurricane Katrina a year ago, which was the most expensive natural disaster in our history. While we cannot say that we see the end of the issues of terrorism or Gulf Coast recovery, it is unacceptable to say that we will let them defeat us.

Going back in time, we no longer die of cholera, which took 10 percent of the lives in Lexington and Russellville in the 1830s. We have not eradicated racism, but we have shattered the laws that shackled a class of our citizens for one hundred years after Appomattox.

Through personal sorrows and efforts to overcome our own shortcomings, many of us have decided that learning to love family and friends as if each day is our last and to serve strangers, as well as those we know, outside oneself is the healing balm for everything.

But just as Daniel Boone wept for his slain son Israel whenever the Battle of Blue Licks was mentioned, just as Jesus wept for Lazarus or a miner's family weeps for the beloved who was lost underground, we will remember and continue to mourn the forty-nine who fell from the sky on Flight 5191.

# Acknowledgements

The title of this book inspired jokes and speculation from friends when it was a work in progress, as in "cured *from* what?" or "cured *as* what?" I leave it to readers to decide. Whatever "the cure," it occurred over many decades of journalism. Readers curious about any more of the story or stories may look in another book, *Wordsmith: My Life in Journalism*, from Clark Legacies and The Pied Type Press, 2011.

Meanwhile, I thank Steve Wrinn of University Press of Kentucky for introducing me to Will McKay of The History Press, which became the publisher of *Kentucky Cured* with Will as editor after scrutiny by Martha Helen.

Other editors had a first go at some of the material, which was originally published in part, in similar or different form in the *Courier-Journal* or *Lexington Herald-Leader*, or both.

My thanks to Keith Runyon of the *Courier-Journal* and Vanessa Gallman of the *Herald-Leader* for accepting pieces by me from which the following chapters were drawn: the *Courier-Journal*—1, 2, 4, 11, 12, 13, 15, 16, 17, 19, 20, 24, 26, 35, 36, 37, 38, 41, 42 and 43; *Lexington Herald-Leader*—8, 9, 10, 13, 14, 18, 22, 25, 26, 28, 32, 33, 34, 40, 41 and 42.

Besides Len Press, who initiated my long stint at KET, old friends from KET who have encouraged or helped me with this book include the present executive director, Shea Hopkins, and her colleague Michelle Ripley. Sid Webb, retired from KET and a skilled photo editor, provided invaluable assistance with the pictures. Tim Bischoff, Steve Shaffer, Bill Goodman and Renee Shaw of KET cheered me on. From the *Herald-Leader* staff came permissions from Peter Baniak and help from Tom Eblen, Jamie Lucke, Cheryl Truman, Ron Garrison and Chris Poore, now at UK. From the *Courier-Journal* I had help from David Hawpe and Tom Loftus and permissions from Mark Taflinger. UK friends who were supportive include Paul Eakin, Dean Terry Birdwhistell and Dean Dan O'Hair, historian Ron Eller, Beth Barnes, Al Cross and Janice Birdwhistell. Janet Whitaker, the veteran KET staffer who later worked at UK, accompanied me on that fruitful visit to Sally Brown.

State historian James Klotter, professor at Georgetown College, as acknowledged in the text, is my great source on all things Kentucky, and attorney Paul Guthrie of Lexington has shared his deep knowledge about World War I.

Betty Carter at the Kentucky Historical Society and Mark Griffin at Logan County Library did valuable picture searches. Tom Noe on the western side of the state found other pictures, as did Linda Gayheart on the east and Allison Webster at University Press of Kentucky. Leslie Page III and Jim Turner, colleagues from the Russellville papers, updated me on Logan County, which I left in 1980. Michal Smith-Mello did some quick research on the Governor Scholars, for which I begged the first dollar from a large corporation in the1980s.

Father Johnnie Ross of Lexington, attorney Steve Cawood of Pineville and reporter Tom Loftus supplied background on several disasters of long ago, which I decided to save for another time, using here just the stories about Hurricane Katrina and Flight 5191. An invitation from Lexington mayor Theresa Isaac and her aides Gerald Smith and Susie Hammonds gave me the opportunity to speak at the community memorial service for victims of Flight 5191 with the thoughts on hope and gratitude that conclude this book. In addition to my children and wife, as noted in the dedication, *Kentucky Cured* is also sent out in grateful memory of all who worked with me in newspapers, radio and television for fifty years. My friends in the recovery community know who they are and that I continue to love them.

# About the Author

Al Smith was born in Sarasota, Florida on January 9, 1927, to parents from middle Tennessee who came to Florida in the early 1920s, attracted by opportunities in that decade's land boom. His father was a war veteran and a lawyer, and his mother had worked as a teenage reporter on a weekly newspaper. Their hopes dashed in the Depression, they returned to Tennessee in 1939 and settled on a rough farm with no amenities near Nashville, acquired with help from family members.

Al's story of his youth in Florida and Tennessee, his own service in the army and life after as a college dropout who became a newspaperman, first in New Orleans and then in Kentucky, is told in *Kentucky Cured* and an earlier memoir, *Wordsmith: My Life in Journalism*, published in 2011.

From a fresh start on a weekly paper in western Kentucky, Al built a chain of small weeklies and a long career in broadcast journalism. Describing himself as a "cause" journalist in and out of the newsroom, he has been an advocate for education, the arts and economic development. The University of Kentucky and eight other colleges and universities have given him honorary doctorates. He lives in Lexington with his wife, Martha Helen, mother of their three adult children.